W9-CJC-926

Jerusalem 1913

Also by Amy Dockser Marcus

The View from Nebo: How Archaeology Is Rewriting the Bible and Reshaping the Middle East

Jerusalem 1913

THE ORIGINS OF THE ARAB-ISRAELI CONFLICT

Amy Dockser Marcus

Viking

VIKING
Published by the Penguin Group
Penguin Group (USA) Inc., 375 Hudson Street, New York, New York 10014, U.S.A.
Penguin Group (Canada), 90 Eglinton Avenue East, Suite 700, Toronto, Ontario,
Canada M4P 2Y3 (a division of Pearson Penguin Canada Inc.)
Penguin Books Ltd, 80 Strand, London WC2R 0RL, England
Penguin Ireland, 25 St. Stephen's Green, Dublin 2, Ireland (a division of Penguin Books Ltd)
Penguin Books Australia Ltd, 250 Camberwell Road, Camberwell, Victoria 3124, Australia
(a division of Pearson Australia Group Pty Ltd)
Penguin Books India Pvt Ltd, 11 Community Centre, Panchsheel Park,
New Delhi – 110 017, India
Penguin Group (NZ), 67 Apollo Drive, Mairangi Bay, Auckland 1311, New Zealand
(a division of Pearson New Zealand Ltd.)
Penguin Books (South Africa) (Pty) Ltd, 24 Sturdee Avenue, Rosebank, Johannesburg 2196,
South Africa

Penguin Books Ltd, Registered Offices: 80 Strand, London WC2R 0RL, England

First published in 2007 by Viking Penguin, a member of Penguin Group (USA) Inc.

10 9 8 7 6 5 4 3 2 1

PHOTOGRAPH CREDITS: Introduction: Library of Congress, Prints and Photographs Division
(#06623) · Jerusalem 1898: Central Zionist Archives · Jerusalem 1908: Library of Congress,
Prints and Photographs Division (#06568) · Jerusalem 1913: Library of Congress, Prints
and Photographs Division (#06546) · Jerusalem 1914: Library of Congress, Prints and
Photographs Division (#02226) · Jerusalem 2004–2006: Library of Congress, Prints and
Photographs Division (#06804)

LIBRARY OF CONGRESS CATALOGING IN PUBLICATION DATA
Marcus, Amy Dockser.
    Jerusalem 1913 : the origins of the Arab-Israeli conflict / Amy Dockser Marcus.
        p. cm.
    Includes index.
    ISBN 978-0-670-03836-7
    1. Arab-Israeli conflict.   2. Palestine—History—20th century.
    3. Israel—History.   I. Title.
    DS119.7.M2935   2007
    956.04—dc22   2006052828

Printed in the United States of America

For Eden, my garden of delight
For Yuval, my brook of joy

Contents

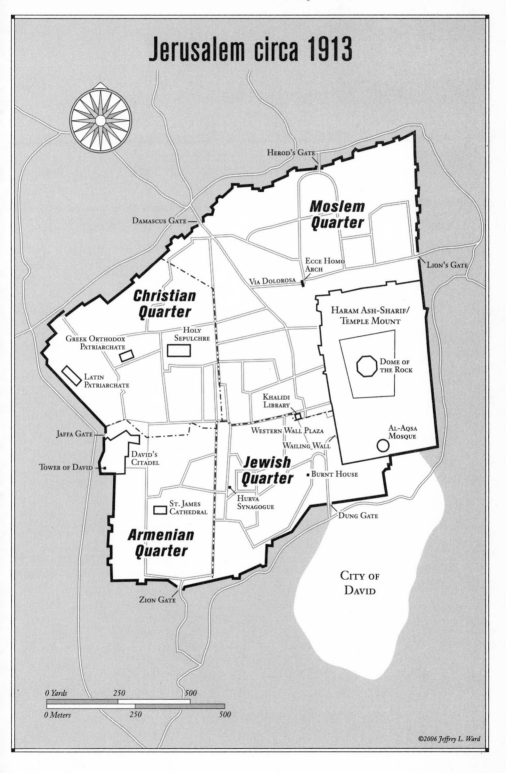

Jerusalem circa 1913

HEROD'S GATE

Moslem Quarter

DAMASCUS GATE

ECCE HOMO ARCH

LION'S GATE

VIA DOLOROSA

Christian Quarter

HARAM ASH-SHARIF/
TEMPLE MOUNT

GREEK ORTHODOX
PATRIARCHATE

HOLY
SEPULCHRE

DOME OF
THE ROCK

LATIN
PATRIARCHATE

KHALIDI
LIBRARY

JAFFA GATE

WESTERN WALL PLAZA

AL-AQSA
MOSQUE

WAILING WALL

TOWER OF DAVID

DAVID'S
CITADEL

Jewish
Quarter

BURNT HOUSE

ST. JAMES
CATHEDRAL

HURVA
SYNAGOGUE

DUNG GATE

Armenian
Quarter

CITY OF
DAVID

ZION GATE

| 0 Yards | 250 | 500 |
| 0 Meters | 250 | 500 |

©2006 Jeffrey L. Ward

Jerusalem 2004–2006

The past is never dead. It's not even past.

—WILLIAM FAULKNER

In September 1991, I flew to Tel Aviv, Israel. I had begun working in New York City three years earlier at *The Wall Street Journal*, first as an entry-level news assistant whose main job was to create charts to illustrate the feature stories that other reporters wrote, and then, for the last two years, as a reporter myself on the legal beat. Every morning on my way in to work, before the day filled with meetings with lawyers or trips to the courthouse to sift through documents and pore over musty court filings, I would stop first in the indoor garden built inside a sleek tower connected to the *Journal*'s main offices by a glass corridor. Sitting on the cold marble stairs, I had a sweeping view of the Hudson River beyond and the garden's palm trees, their height and grace an incongruous sight in a downtown Manhattan complex. They were a constant reminder of warmer foreign climes.

Since the age of seven, I had spent part of each summer in Jerusalem, the city where my parents had first met while spending time there in the early 1960s, and to which they continually returned after they married. As a child, the side streets of Jerusalem had felt as comfortable to me as our own neighborhood back home.

During those mornings staring at the palm trees before work started, I dreamed of going back, this time as a foreign correspondent. Like other young reporters at *The Wall Street Journal*, I was eager to find a way to get on the front page. But I also felt the pull of the city itself, with its dramatic history and sweeping beauty. It had always been a place about which I felt I had something to say.

Since speaking one of the languages of the region seemed like a good way to begin, I had been trudging every Sunday morning for two years to an intensive Hebrew-language class. I had studied Hebrew as a child, but still could not speak fluently. The class was taught by a young woman not long out of the Israeli army, and she ran the course with no-nonsense efficiency and an air of command. Her husband was studying at one of the New York universities, and she spoke longingly about going back to their neighborhood outside Tel Aviv, where many of the residents traced their roots to Iraq, and where the constant aromas of the women cooking traditional foods followed you down the street. She described the way the women hung their wet laundry on lines strung across the porch, the bright colors like lines of flags representing different countries, and how the older men whiled away the evening playing backgammon, the clicking of the dice and the cadences of their voices coming through the open windows as she prepared dinner for her children.

We were an odd assortment of students—retired men and women on pensions who seemed as if they had been looking for a reason to get out of the house, Holocaust survivors who spoke Hebrew with heavy accents and a sense of pride, a beautiful aspiring soap opera actress who was dating an Israeli and working as a waitress while she went to auditions, young couples planning on moving to Israel. The teacher allowed no English to be spoken; if you wanted to say something and couldn't think of the word in Hebrew, she insisted on pantomime. That class is how I came to meet my husband, an Israeli who had come to New York to attend college. He was working his way through school as a security guard, checking our identification as we entered the building where the class was held. A year later, we married.

By the summer of 1991, as the first Persian Gulf War came to an end, the *Journal* no longer had a correspondent based in Israel; instead, it had been flying in reporters from London to cover major events. Many of the paper's editors believed that the potential for peace between Israel and the Arab world had ground to a halt. Now, in the wake of the war, there was talk that the United States saw a unique opportunity to try to remake the Middle East, and resolving the Arab-Israeli conflict would constitute a major part of this effort. I asked the managing editor to give me a chance to cover this process on the ground, and he agreed. If the stalemate continued and there was no political change, we decided, I would return home.

One day soon after I arrived, while exploring one of the areas damaged by missiles from the war in a town outside Tel Aviv, I bumped into my Hebrew teacher from New York walking down the street. By that time, her husband had finished school, and they had moved back with their children to Israel. I was surprised to discover that the neighborhood about which she had regaled us with stories back in New York was the same one where I was now walking.

Many Israelis that I knew had been forced to sit out the war in bomb shelters or "sealed rooms" that they prepared at home with duct tape and plastic sheeting, wearing gas masks in case of chemical attack and waiting for code words on the radio that would indicate it was safe to take them off. The United States, which had led the struggle against Saddam Hussein, feared that its fragile coalition of Arab states against Iraq's invasion of Kuwait might fall apart if the Israelis joined. The United States extracted a promise from then Israeli prime minister Yitzhak Shamir that Israel would try to stay out of the conflict, even if attacked by Scud missiles. That agreement had only added to the strange uncertainty that seemed to permeate everything during that period, for each time the Scuds hit Tel Aviv, Israelis wondered if Shamir would go back on his word. The lack of response to the Scud attacks seemed counter to the ethos that had driven Israel forward since its founding.

And yet by the fall of 1991, life more or less had returned to normal. The coffee shops were full, the nightclubs were crowded, the steady beat of daily routine went on, even amid the signs of damage.

Within a few months of the end of hostilities, elections were held, and Yitzhak Rabin, the famed general and hero of the 1967 Arab-Israeli war, which had resulted in Israel's capture of the West Bank and the Gaza Strip and the reunification of the eastern and western parts of Jerusalem, was chosen as prime minister. Soon afterward he became involved in secret negotiations with representatives of the Palestine Liberation Organization, which culminated in the 1993 signing of the Oslo peace accords—named after the Norwegian capital where most of the talks had taken place—and a formal ceremony on the White House lawn. At first, following the famous handshake between Rabin and PLO leader Yasser Arafat, it was a time of optimism. Everyone, Israelis and Palestinians alike, seemed to be signing a deal—to sell tomatoes to the Persian Gulf, to look for oil in the Dead Sea, to open a casino in Jericho. There was talk of a new Middle East, the falling of borders, and an era of open trade. The Tel Aviv cafés always seemed to be full of people talking business.

It is hard to pinpoint when things started going wrong. Looking back on that period now, I see the turning point as November 1995, when Yitzhak Rabin was killed by a Jewish right-wing militant following a peace demonstration in Tel Aviv. The image of Rabin's closest aide—red-eyed from crying, unshaven and unkempt after an all-night vigil—announcing outside the hospital in a trembling voice that Rabin had died, became a symbol for me of all the dashed expectations. It was the end of an era.

When new elections were held Benjamin Netanyahu of the Likud Party became prime minister, promising to change what he considered Rabin's foolhardy commitment to the Oslo accords. Conflicts between the Israeli army and the Palestinians continued in the West Bank and the Gaza Strip, and a new kind of terrorism gripped Israel—suicide bombing. Today, reports of suicide bombings throughout the world are common—in the subway in London, on a bus in Iraq, in a hotel frequented by tourists in Bali—but a decade ago, it was a shockingly novel act of violence. I would be walking somewhere—on the way to the supermarket, to attend a lecture at a museum, going to meet and interview a source—when suddenly a news bulletin would burst over the radio to report that a Palestinian militant had blown himself up on a bus or detonated himself in the middle of a crowd. The next day newspapers always featured pictures of the fatalities, tiny, grainy photos with black-bordered edges from someone's national identification card, or sometimes candid pictures of happier times supplied by the families of the victims.

The bombing I remember most vividly took place on Friday, March 21, 1997. It was the Jewish holiday of Purim, which commemorates the miraculous escape of the Jews from the evil plans of the king of Persia's adviser Haman, who wanted to kill them all. In Israel, it has always been a huge and festive celebration, with adults and children dressing up in costumes, parades held in virtually every town, and children feasting on candy and attending raucous outdoor fairs. I was preparing to go into Tel Aviv to one of the parades with my daughter, who was five months old at the time. I had dressed her up as Minnie Mouse, and I remember thinking that the costume felt stiff, the crinoline puffing up at the bottom of the red-and-white polka-dot dress and scratching me as I got her ready. We were walking through the center of the suburb where we lived, just eight miles north of Tel Aviv, enjoying the fine weather and the sight of so many people we knew wearing masks and costumes, when suddenly a hush seemed to settle on the entire street.

The radio announcer broke in to announce that at 1:45 p.m. that day, a twenty-eight-year-old Palestinian had walked into a popular Tel Aviv restaurant called Café Apropo. He tried to get a seat inside, but because it was packed with revelers for the holiday he couldn't find an empty table. The waitress showed him to a place on the terrace, where moments after he sat down he detonated a bomb in his bag. Three women at nearby tables were killed, and forty-eight people wounded.

In the nearly six years that I had been living in Israel, terrorist attacks had become a fact of life. Some of them I covered as a reporter, interviewing the victims, trying to find the family members of the perpetrators, chronicling an endless cycle of revenge and destruction. I no longer gave a second thought to the armed guards who checked my purse every time I ran into the supermarket to buy milk. I'd grown used to every package I received in the mail being stamped with a warning not to open it if it seemed suspicious. When I saw an unattended bag in a hotel lobby, I knew to report it to a guard.

And yet, in the days following the Café Apropo attack, I sat riveted to the television, horrified by one image that was replayed again and again: a distraught policewoman cradling an injured baby outside the destroyed restaurant. That image haunted me in a way that coverage of previous terror attacks had not. The baby, Shani Winter, was six months old, a month older than my own daughter. Café Apropo was just a few blocks from the office where my husband worked as an architect. Sometimes, on the way back from a press conference or a meeting in Jerusalem, I had asked the cab driver to drop me off there and my husband and I had sat on that very terrace to drink a cup of coffee together before going home.

Nothing was ever quite the same for me after that bombing. For a time I stopped going to outdoor restaurants in Tel Aviv, preferring to eat at home or at restaurants outside the city. I no longer took my daughter with me to crowded places like the mall. I started to turn over in my mind one key question: *How had this happened?*

I didn't mean the practical aspects of the attack, which over the ensuing weeks were laid out in precise detail in the Israeli press—the path the bomber had followed, the people who had recruited him and provided him with the bomb, those who had aided him in his journey that landed him in that restaurant in Tel Aviv. Rather, I was thinking much more broadly, pondering the violence, the carnage, the inability to see the other as a human being. Had it always been this way? At any moment along the path that had brought us to this point, could things have turned out differently?

I was not the first to wonder about the roots of this enmity. The Arab-Israeli conflict is not the legacy of millennia of hostility. Given that Zionist settlement in Palestine did not even begin until the end of the nineteenth century, the dispute is 125 years old, at the most. When the first Jewish settlers arrived in Palestine in the late 1880s with the goal of reclaiming Zion, the Ottomans had ruled the area for over four hundred years. Their hegemony ended in 1917, when the British army marched in and took over Jerusalem, the British soldiers accepting the surrender of the Ottomans in the garden of a Jerusalem hospital.

Most attempts to unravel the start of the conflict trace it back to that period, the time of the British Mandate, which officially began in 1920 and ended with Britain's pullout from Palestine in 1948. In many ways, this is a sensible approach. There is no doubt that in the twenty-eight years of the Mandate period, the conflict that continues to dominate headlines today and fuels tensions in the wider Middle East became increasingly contentious. The Mandate ended with the outbreak of the first Arab-Israeli war, what the Israelis call the War of Independence because it began after the announcement of the creation of the modern state of Israel in 1948. A national army took to the battlefield, the Israelis emerged victorious, and Palestinians were displaced from their homes, becoming the refugees that many still remain even today.

Still, this intense focus on the Mandate period did not seem to offer a full picture, for by the time the 1948 war broke out, both parties were already too fully in opposition for the end to be anything but a full-scale war. Why had so little attention been paid to the earlier Ottoman era, when the two sides had lived in relative peace, when they had shared the same community and set of common experiences, when they saw themselves for better or worse as being part of the same group?

From the time I had arrived in Israel, I had been drawn to Jerusalem, in particular the part known as the Old City, its ancient core. There I could see the remains of each epoch of its history, piled one on top of the other, as one group came in and built upon what the previous generation had left behind. I had walked through the cobblestoned alleyways with a friend who knew every inch of the city, and as we made our way, she would point out a stone foundation dating from the Ottoman period, a beautiful Mamluk-era façade, a Roman arch, a tower King Herod built, an Abbasid vault, a Canaanite cornerstone. From these traces of the past, the outlines of an alternative narrative to the one that now dominated the news began to emerge. There had been a time when the various groups shared the city, when they saw this place as their common homeland. You could not help but wonder, when confronted with this amazing heritage, about what had gone wrong. How did a place with such a rich history of ethnic diversity become so divided by sectarian conflict? And when had it happened?

2

In May 1913, a Russian filmmaker named Noah Sokolovsky arrived in Palestine, planning to make a movie about the Jewish settlements there. A devastating war was only a year away, and the world was teetering on the edge of a conflagration the likes of which it had not experienced before. Even those who could not fully imagine what lay ahead knew that a great change was inevitable. Sokolovsky wanted to make sure that he documented the Jewish enterprise in Palestine before it, too, was transformed.

By 1913, news about the Zionist movement's work in Palestine was well known to Russian Jews like Sokolovsky. In fact, it was Russian Jews who then formed the backbone of the settlement movement, packing lectures about life in Palestine given by Menachem Ussishkin and other Russian-born Zionist leaders, and pooling their money in order to buy growing numbers of plots of land in Tel Aviv. They had contributed so much to help the Jewish National Fund obtain land that negotiations were soon under way to buy a beautiful plot on a hill with a commanding view of Jerusalem, which it was hoped would be the future site of the first national Jewish university in Palestine. (In 1918 the cornerstone was laid for what is today the Hebrew University in Jerusalem.)

Sokolovsky went everywhere around the country in May and June of 1913, filming what he saw and, more important, what he wanted others to see. He traveled to Tel Aviv and to Haifa, he visited the Wailing Wall in Jerusalem, and he followed penitents up to the seventh stair outside the cave where Abraham was believed to be buried in Hebron, the highest step to which Jews could ascend before being barred by the Muslim caretakers of the shrine. What he saw and observed during his journey amazed and delighted him. Throughout the film he shot, there is an almost palpable energy, a pulsing nationalism that did not need words or sound to vividly express itself.

Sokolovsky worked very quickly, wrapping up the filming a month after it began, in June 1913. He returned to Russia to compile and edit, and took the finished work to Vienna a few months later, in September 1913, to present it to standing-room-only crowds at the annual Zionist Congress meeting. This was the last congress before the onset of World War I, and so Sokolovsky's movie debut would soon be forgotten amid subsequent events. When future historians wrote about that conference, what they chose to emphasize was Chaim Weizmann's speech about the planned Hebrew University in Jerusalem, and the 25,000-person-strong pilgrimage to Theodor Herzl's gravesite during one of the breaks in the proceedings.

Despite its popularity at the conference, however, Sokolovsky's movie had been criticized by a number of people who worried about the vision it portrayed, a complaint that would be leveled in one form or another about the Zionist movement itself over the ensuing years. The film focused too much on the Jews, the critics said. You would never have guessed from the movie that anyone but Jews lived in Jaffa and Haifa, where vibrant Arab communities comprised the majority. The Jewish settlers were at the forefront of every scene, and it was often hard to distinguish anything or anyone else. Still, these were minor complaints in the overall enthusiastic response, and after its successful opening at the Zionist Congress the film made the rounds in Polish and Russian Jewish communities over the following year. When World War I broke out in August 1914, all signs—and apparently all copies—of the film soon vanished, lost amid the tumult of the war years and the upheaval arising from the carnage of that conflict.

Most people had long forgotten about *The Life of the Jews in Palestine*, as the film had been known, when in 1997 a researcher stumbled upon its original negative at the French national film archives. Here before the eyes of those who viewed it was a long-lost world, restored back to life. The French recognized its historical importance and contacted colleagues in Israel. In collaboration with Israeli researchers who scoured Zionist movement archives, both in Jerusalem and in Poland, they tried to find any written original material related to the movie and the events that it recorded. Working from what they found and the negative itself, the team of researchers managed to reconstruct the film. The new version was aired with great fanfare on Israeli television and then, almost in a repeat of its first incarnation, made the rounds of Jewish film festivals around the world. Inevitably a certain amount of nostalgia accompanied each viewing of the film, for the world that it had recorded no longer existed, and the life of the Jews in Palestine was vastly different from what it had been back in 1913.

Knowing of my interest in that era, Israeli friends who had seen the movie urged me to view it. One day in 2000 on a visit back to Jerusalem, I went to the Israel Broadcasting headquarters and asked someone to dig through the video archives to find it.

Viewing the film was a disconcerting experience. In Israel that year, the conflict between the Israelis and the Palestinians seemed as intractable as ever. The intense violence, which never totally abated, had surged again with a horrifying round of terrorist attacks and military strikes, suicide bombings and drive-by shootings. There never seemed to be a moment of peace or stillness. And yet here, before my eyes on the television screen, set to the kind of accordion-dominated musical background familiar from Jewish weddings, were the flickering images of another, more hopeful time, before all of the present conflict had begun.

Other than the soundtrack that had been added to it, the film was silent: no commentary, no narrative, no re-creation of the voices of the characters as they might have spoken when they were filmed going about their daily lives. Only a series of quick introductory placards succinctly oriented the viewer. I watched as people with long coats trudged up a gangplank in Odessa to board a boat that would take them to Jaffa, bearing a heavy burden not only of musical instrument cases, bulging packages, and ramshackle suitcases bursting with old clothes, but also their ambitions and dreams about the uncertain future that lay ahead in Palestine.

Here before my eyes emerged the shape of Jewish life in Palestine in 1913, and with it a growing realization: every conflict had a turning point, a moment when things could have gone a little differently, when choices were made or decisions postponed, and from this turning point emerged a cascade of consequences, a narrowing of further options, and the path that had led us to today. It seemed that 1913 held many of the answers to my efforts to understand what was hap-pening in our own time in Israel and with the Arab-Israeli conflict.

In viewing the movie in this light, it was evident that some of what I was searching for was not always at the center of Sokolovsky's camera lens, but often off to the side, at the corner of his frame. In one of the opening scenes, he films the boat bearing the new im-migrants to Palestine as it makes its way through the Bosporous on the way to Jaffa. Sailboats go by, their triangular sails fanning out, and the tiered buildings of Constantinople press toward the sea as if they might topple into it at any moment. And then, just for a mo-ment, the camera pans across a massive warship anchored at sea but clearly within easy range of Constantinople—one of the ships sent by Britain, France, and the other European countries as a reminder to the Ottoman Empire that it was being watched, a constant hover-ing threat that the empire's days were numbered. Once the film moves to Palestine, a similar feeling prevails, a sense that the future, the conflict to come, is right there at the edge of things.

In one respect, I had never understood the criticism of Soko-lovsky's work. He had never intended to provide straightforward reportage or presented himself as an objective commentator. He had come to Palestine on a mission, and it was clear from the outset that his goal was to make a propaganda film. He had undertaken the task at the behest of the Zionist movement, and he had gone to Je-rusalem, Haifa, and other cities in Palestine to capture the reality of Jewish life there, but only a selective reality. In the limits of the scope of his project, there was an important message.

At the 1913 Zionist Congress, the very one at which the film was screened night after night for the eager delegates, Arthur Ruppin, the head of the Palestine Office in Jaffa, gave one of the most impor-tant speeches of his career. The Palestine Office was the operating arm of the Zionist movement in Palestine, and many of the images of settlements, new schools, thriving enterprises, and earnest Zionist endeavors featured in the film were the result of projects that Ruppin had either funded or supported or in which he was somehow personally involved.

At the Congress, sometimes in formal sessions but often in casual conversations during breaks, delegates were already discussing the growing conflict with the Arabs in Palestine. In fact, Ruppin and many others in the Zionist movement were already involved in what can only be described as the first Arab-Jewish peace negotiations over the future of Palestine. But in his speech, Ruppin made no mention of these talks, instead articulating for the first time a topic that until then had been hidden or confined to memos that only a small group of the most devoted activists had been permitted to read. In his speech to the delegates in Vienna, Ruppin stated directly what the movie was showing them in images: namely, that Jews should attempt to become the majority in Palestine. They should fill every frame of the picture. If they wanted their culture, their language, their schools, and ultimately their army to be dominant, there was no other way. Things were changing rapidly, Ruppin argued. You only had to see Sokolovsky's movie to understand that the warships already sat on the Bosporus at the entrance to Constantinople and weren't going away. The competition for land in Palestine was well under way. The key question that was about to be decided was: Who would ultimately control Palestine?

Noah Sokolovsky's film offered one compelling version of the answer. The filmmaker had worked diligently to demonstrate and reinforce the Jewish religious and historical attachment to the land, including footage of the tombs of Absalom, Zechariah, and Rachel, along with those of various rabbis and mystics. He crosscut the biblical and historical images with vivid pictures of the modern life in Palestine that the Jews who had returned there had started to build. He cut from Hasidic worshippers headed for prayers at the Wailing Wall in Jerusalem to farmers on the main street of the Jewish settlement of Hadera, their horse-drawn carriages struggling to get around the knots of women balancing heavy packages on their heads and the camels loaded with goods ambling down the street. One moment a viewer might watch religious students bent over the Torah in a school next to a biblical site; the next, shots of farmers picking almonds and packing oranges into crates to be sold abroad. Sokolovsky saw these images as being connected, and wanted his viewers to do so as well.

Later in the movie appears Meir Dizengoff, mayor of the new city of Tel Aviv, which Ruppin had helped create and had insisted should be built with wider than normal streets because he felt it would someday be the commercial center of a Jewish entity. Dizengoff is surrounded by a knot of men wearing straw boaters and planning the future of Palestine. Sokolovsky also included picture after picture of a line of girls, their long dark hair tied back in ribbons, pressed white smocks gleaming, skirts reaching down to their ankles, as they march in pairs holding hands in their Jaffa schoolyard. They are taking part in an agriculture lesson, planting tiny seedlings and then energetically hacking away at the dirt with their hoes as the filmmaker chronicles their dedicated labor. At one point in the movie, they tilt their heads back to the sun in unison as they line up for calisthenics. The images of the girls are followed by lines of men in white shorts doing gymnastic exercises, running and jumping and hoisting their bodies on the pommel horse or the parallel bars. Many of them wear small fezzes, which stay firmly perched on their heads despite their strenuous physical exertions. They run in synchronized fashion, each man shooting forward, exuding strength and control, power and discipline.

The Life of the Jews in Palestine's penultimate scene records an outdoor ceremony on the sand dunes at the outskirts of Tel Aviv, as people gather to celebrate the rapid creation of the new town, the remarkable growth it has undergone in a short time, and its prosperous future. For a moment, the camera turns away from the center of the festivities and catches the image of several men, their heads wrapped in traditional Arab headdresses called kaffiyehs, standing apart from the others, looking on from the edge of the dancing circle. They appear to be older than the celebrants, and by their dress and manner are most likely Arabs from Jaffa or a nearby village. Although the camera moves on quickly, the viewer cannot help but notice their impassivity, how they watch and wait with intense stares. It is impossible to know what they might have been thinking. Were they looking beyond the sand dunes, where the future stretched? At that moment, it was still a blank slate, fresh and unmarked. Anything seemed possible. And yet the celebration has become so exuberant that the boisterous dancers are already straying across the line of the dunes and into the emptiness beyond, where nothing has yet been built. Their stomping feet leave traces of their progress in the smooth white sand.

3

The rediscovery of *The Life of the Jews in Palestine* took place during a surge of interest in and nostalgia for the history of Israel. With the upsurge in violence in the country starting in 2000, people seemed more eager to escape into the past than to think about the present or the future. Clubs that specialized in Israeli folk songs, written mainly about the early days of the state's existence and a staple of most Israelis' childhoods, now were packed night after night with audiences who seemed to want to revel in their memories. Israelis would plan a night out with large groups of friends, filling row after row of large, picnic-style tables, singing along with whichever faded folksinger was featured that night. Sometimes, as the evening wore on, they would push the tables close together, link arms, and stretch from one end of the club to the other, performing truncated, drunken versions of Israeli folk dances.

One popular radio program of the time, which broadcast on Friday afternoons, when the pace of life in Israel slowed down and the beginning of the Jewish Sabbath and weekend got under way, was dedicated to old books: character series, adventures, books that Israelis had enjoyed as children and now suddenly felt the urge to locate and read again. The host of the program, who also ran a secondhand bookstore in a suburb north of Tel Aviv where cats wandered freely through the aisles, took calls from listeners. They would ask him to find a particular book, and would always recount with a mixture of pride and wistfulness the story behind their request, the emotions and memories that the book evoked. There was a sense that people longed for the past because then, at least, things had seemed clear. Now, with the unremitting violence and the confusion over how to stop it, there was a hopelessness, almost a feeling of bewilderment. The retreat to the past was fueled by the belief that things had somehow been better back then.

The Ottoman era seemed like the most obvious period to study if you were trying to trace the origins of the conflict that would play a key role in Israel's future. It was the last time the Arabs and Jews had a shared, joint history, when the two sides lived together in relative peace. But for a long time, it held little fascination for scholars, historians, or most of the general public. For both Palestinians and Israelis, the Ottoman era was viewed as one of the low points in the history of the country. Disagreeing on so much about the present, they nonetheless shared the belief that the Ottoman rule was a time of desolation, unremitting poverty, and deep political oppression.

In his book *Between Past and Present*, Neil Asher Silberman, an archaeological historian, describes a visit he made years earlier to a gift shop in David's Citadel, one of the most popular tourist sites in

Jerusalem. Located just inside the Jaffa Gate leading to the Old City, the Citadel is one of the most familiar landmarks of the city skyline—jutting above the Old City's wall, it appears to stand guard over Jerusalem. Despite its name, the structure itself dates to the Mamluk-Ottoman time, and was probably built in the fourteenth to sixteenth centuries, although the foundation of the building was constructed even earlier. There are six towers in the Citadel, the oldest of which was built by King Herod, and it survived the destruction of Jerusalem and the Second Temple in 70 AD only because the Roman conquerors wanted people to see the formidable defensive structures its army had breached and spared it. The tower known as David's Citadel or the Tower of David had actually served as a mosque and was topped by a minaret. The Ottoman soldiers who stood guard there used it as their house of prayer.

David's Citadel is now a popular museum where visitors go from room to room, tower to tower, learning about Jerusalem's past. Sometimes concerts are held in its courtyard, and at night its walls are illuminated. On the day that Silberman visited, his eye was caught by a basket on the counter of the gift shop next to the cash register. It contained red- and gray-mottled pottery fragments, remnants of smoking pipes that had been found during archaeological excavations of the Citadel and were now on sale to any tourist who happened to visit. Silberman recounted how these pipes had been mass-produced during the Ottoman era and sold throughout the region. In excavations, they had often been discarded, a piece of history now reduced to a tourist trinket. It outraged Silberman that no one appreciated their value as vessels containing historical information about an overlooked time. The presence of the pipes there, he argued, was a symbol of a greater problem—the willful forgetfulness, the unacceptable ignorance, that Israelis as well as Palestinians had about the Ottoman past. Both sides preferred to disregard the Ottoman era, while they should be mining it for clues about how they became who they are today, how they ended up locked in such a bitter, bloody struggle.

In recent years, this indifference has given way to a new appreciation for the relevance of the Ottoman period in any consideration of the Middle East. Israeli scholars interested in reconstructing the history of Zionist settlement in Palestine started examining Ottoman court records, family papers, oral histories, and personal correspondence to try to learn more about the background against which the earliest phase of the Zionist movement had taken place. Palestinian scholars, who wanted to reclaim their own history, also turned their attention to the Ottoman era as a critical period before the onset of Israeli rule. Soon histories of individual towns like Jericho, Bir Zeit, and al-Taybeh were being published. One scholar of Palestinian history, Baruch Kimmerling, estimated that three-quarters of the present-day Palestinians were descendants of people who had lived in the Jerusalem *sanjak*, or administrative district, comprising Jerusalem and its surrounding environs, during Ottoman rule; understanding life in that *sanjak*, in turn, was seen to be a key in understanding the emergence of a separate Palestinian identity.

Even archaeologists, who had traditionally chosen to focus on the biblical period or the Crusades, regarding these as most deeply connected to Western civilization and identity, started reassessing the Ottoman era, and stopped discarding those clay pipes or selling them at gift shops. Palestinian archaeologists launched a dig to recover Ottoman-period artifacts in the Palestinian village of Ti'innik, located adjacent to the biblical-era site of Tannach. Some believed that Palestinian peasant life during that epoch might offer insights into more ancient practices of agriculture, perhaps even dating back to biblical times. Palestinians started collecting modern pottery made by local village potters, in an attempt to link their patterns and styles further back in time to older relics, some from biblical-era sites.

Uzi Baram, an archaeologist born in Israel but now living in the

United States, told me when we met in Jerusalem that he hoped to spearhead and nurture the growing interest in the archaeology of the Ottoman period. In 1998 he helped organize and run a conference in New York, inviting scholars—Palestinians, Israelis, and Americans among them—who wanted to jump-start archaeological exploration of this era to share their findings from digs around the former provinces of the Ottoman Empire. Later, Baram and his colleagues collated the key papers and presentations from the conference into a book. In the introduction he and his colleague Lynda Carroll wrote for it, they discussed the political implications they discerned in the growing respect for the Ottoman legacy. That research, they wrote, "has the potential for aiding in rethinking the past for Israelis and Palestinians." Someone who rethinks the past, they added, is more likely to contemplate different paths for the future, as well.

4

This book's title is *Jerusalem 1913*, but the story that it chronicles actually opens fifteen years earlier, in 1898, the year that Theodor Herzl made his first and only trip to Palestine. Despite being considered the father of the Zionist movement, Herzl made the journey to Palestine unwillingly and had never shown much interest in traveling there. As a former playwright and working journalist, he had always preferred sojourns in European cities, preferably ones with good food and an interesting nightlife. His life changed dramatically in 1894, however, when Captain Alfred Dreyfus, the only Jew serving on the French army general staff, was charged with spying for Germany. At the time, Herzl was writing for a Viennese newspaper and was present in the courtroom during the only two days of the Dreyfus trial for which the public was allowed to witness the proceedings. His background research had convinced him that Dreyfus was innocent of the charges, a victim of the anti-Semitism that had grown increasingly public in Europe during this period. Dreyfus was ultimately found guilty and stripped of his rank, and Herzl found himself haunted by the crowds screaming "Death to the Jews" after the verdict was announced, their virulent response only confirming his convictions about the prevalence of anti-Jewish sentiment.

For a time, he stopped going out with friends, barely ate, and, unable to sleep, spent long, feverish nights thinking about the Dreyfus affair and its implications. He reflected upon his own life experiences, and those of his friends, whose careers had stalled after a certain point for seemingly inexplicable reasons—reasons he now saw as part of a larger pattern of discrimination. He became convinced that the only solution to anti-Semitism was to create a place where Jews could be the majority and forge their own nation. Herzl wasn't sure Palestine was the right choice at first, but there was already a nascent Zionist movement in Russia rallying around these ideas. Political pragmatism made Herzl realize that Palestine was the choice most likely to win the broadest support.

In 1897 Herzl published his ideas in a short political manifesto entitled *The Jewish State*, which had an enormous influence on the shape of life in Jerusalem in later years. Even though Herzl had only visited Jerusalem once, many of the structures that he described in that work as avenues for executing his political vision—a bank, a Zionist Congress, an administrative arm to buy land—actually came into being in the years following the manifesto's publication. Some of them, including the Palestine Office, the Jewish National Fund, and the Zionist Congress, dominated the events and decisions of 1913 and could not have been realized without Herzl's foresight.

Herzl's life did not have a happy ending; he died young, in pain from a heart condition, isolated from his wife and children. His three children all came to deeply troubled ends—his son converted to several different religions, one after another, and then committed suicide shortly after learning of the death of his drug-addicted sister; a third child, Trude, died in a Nazi concentration camp. Herzl's trip to Jerusalem took place at what people would later realize was the end of an era.

But if Herzl's journey establishes the themes of this book, it was the Young Turk revolution of 1908 that defines them. In that year a group of young, ambitious Ottoman army officers, dissatisfied with the way the empire was being run, disillusioned by the corruption and cronyism of the sultan's ruling clique, and chafing for a chance themselves to rule, took over the government. Their coup made possible everything that followed afterward in Palestine, for though both Jewish and Arab nationalism had existed before the Young Turks took over, the new constitution they promulgated and the air of freedom they inspired made it possible, at least initially, for the Jews and the Arabs to imagine themselves as the creators of their own destinies. Newspapers and journals that both reported on and criticized the Ottoman government—and that also closely followed and described the emerging Arab-Zionist conflict—came into existence in the years after 1908.

The heart of the book concerns the events of 1913, the year that I came to see as a crucial turning point. It is never easy, even with the benefit of hindsight, to pinpoint a month, a year, when history witnesses a defining moment. Any good scholar—and there have been many who have written seminal academic books about various aspects of this period—can marshal evidence to argue that it was two years earlier or four years later or a completely different point in time. But in choosing 1913 as my focus, I realized that what happened that year more than any other answered the question that had bothered me during my time living in Israel: Why had things gone wrong?

It was in 1913, at the last Zionist Congress to be held until after World War I, that Zionist leader after Zionist leader stood up and argued that they must aspire to create both cultural and demographic domination in Palestine. By 1913, plans were in place for more Jewish communities and settlements there, the rise of Hebrew as a national language was well under way, and the formation of an infrastructure that would form the skeleton of a state had already emerged. Military groups had also begun to coalesce, groups that eventually formed the nucleus of the nascent Israeli army. In 1913, Jews and Palestinians undertook the serious effort to negotiate what we today would call a Middle East peace agreement, and the reasons why those negotiations failed involved many of the same issues and problems that still undermine our efforts to find a way for the two sides to reconcile. In 1913, more than at any other time, choices that were made set both parties down a particular path that slowly but inexorably led to where they stand today.

In writing this book, I chose to focus on Jerusalem, because Jerusalem then as now stood at the center of things. Even Herzl, who instinctively recoiled from the dirt and the noise and the ethnic fluidity of the city, still found himself drawn to it during his visit there, almost against his will. It was a place where Jews had always maintained a presence and where Muslims, Jews, and Christians mixed together, fought, competed, argued, and shared their lives. In telling the story of 1913, I have tried to see it through the eyes of its people, who were transformed by the events of that year and were forced for the first time to take sides.

In my research as I sought to find the narrative voices for the book, I found myself intrigued by several figures: Albert Antebi, a Jew born in Damascus who came to dominate the Jewish community in Jerusalem but never embraced Zionism; Ruhi Khalidi, the scion of a prominent Muslim family that had held important religious and social positions in Jerusalem for years, who found himself on the cusp of an emerging Arab nationalism; and Arthur Ruppin, an ardent Zionist and the only one of the three to live to witness the creation of the state of Israel. In tracing their lives and experiences during that dramatic time, it is possible to mourn a lost world, missed opportunities, and the choices—often made with the best of intentions and for the most understandable of reasons—that would affect the region's destiny.

In June 1913, too, the first Arab-Syrian Congress took place in Paris, and became the backdrop both to furious negotiations between the Arabs and political leaders of the Ottoman Empire about the future of Arab nationalism and to secret talks between the Zionist leaders and Arab nationalists about whether it was possible to share in the rule of Palestine and find common ground. As the conference got started, many people and groups sent congratulatory telegrams and letters of support to its founders and sponsors. One telegram was sent by a group of Arab Americans. Their vision of the future of the Ottoman Empire and the Arabs' role in it was based on their own experiences in America. They proposed that the Ottoman rulers view Constantinople as if it were Washington, D.C., the head of a federal government, but offer Arabs and other groups autonomy and power comparable to that enjoyed by states in the United States. Only with such an arrangement, they argued, would it truly be possible to be both a loyal Ottoman and a proud Arab nationalist.

Amid the tumult of the conference and its aftermath, and the outbreak of a world war a little over a year later, this telegram never received much attention. While a single telegram is certainly not representative of an entire movement or even a powerful individual voice, it does raise questions about other paths that might have been taken. If the Ottoman Empire, or even the nation-states that were carved out of it in the wake of World War I, had been able to offer people a more robust vision of identity, one that would allow them to find a way to express their own ethnic uniqueness, practice their religion and culture, and yet still feel part of a shared homeland and a common identity, could things have gone differently? Was there a way that the damage the two sides have done to each other over the years could have been prevented or, at the very least, ameliorated in some way? Had the Arabs and the Jews not underestimated one another in crucial ways, could their negotiations have been more productive?

But of course, those other paths were not taken. Events unfolded in a certain way, and we have lived with the consequences. Instead of speculating on what might have been, this book was written in an attempt to understand what actually did take place in that crucial year, and how it affected everything that came afterward. In trying to better understand these events, in attempting to show how intertwined the inhabitants of Palestine once were and how and why the social, cultural, and political fabric came undone, there is always the hope that we can see the present more clearly. I also share the quiet idea that in rethinking the past, it is sometimes possible to rethink the future.

When I visit Jerusalem now, I do not only see the crowds of my contemporaries rushing around me. When I walk through the Old City, I imagine Albert Antebi sitting in a coffee shop, joking with his friends, negotiating a deal. I easily conjure up Ruhi Khalidi in his library, books piled around him as he takes notes or jots down his thoughts for another newspaper article. I imagine Arthur Ruppin regaling his friends with tales at a dinner party. I am sure that I can hear the faint sounds of an oud being played all night long by an aspiring musician, or the plaintive notes of an aching melody, wafting from one of the rooftop parties where Muslim, Jewish, and Christian neighbors used to meet and mingle. In the distance is the rising beat of nationalism. It is faint, but growing louder every day. People like Albert Antebi and Ruhi Khalidi can hear it, and have already begun to worry about what it means for themselves and for their city, Jerusalem. Their lament for Jerusalem echoes even today.

PART ONE

Jerusalem 1898

When I remember thee in days to come . . .

—THEODOR HERZL

1

While Theodor Herzl's publication of *The Jewish State* in 1897 had called for a Jewish homeland, it did not specifically name Palestine as the best site for the purpose. Rather, it was the delegates at the first meeting of the Zionist Congress held shortly after the book appeared who insisted on that location. Palestine had been the ancient site of the last Jewish homeland, they argued, and should be that homeland once again. Herzl, realizing that he needed to attract supporters to his cause, quickly rallied to the idea. He even suggested creating popular festivals at the tombs of venerated rabbis in Palestine as a plan for boosting tourism.

Despite Herzl's commitment to the idea of a Jewish state, however, he had not been particularly eager to visit Palestine. He had spent the past year traveling, often shuttling to Basel, Switzerland, where he had set up and then presided over the first Zionist Congress, which attracted 197 supporters from Jewish communities around the world and was held with much pomp in a former gambling hall. His bosses at the prestigious Viennese newspaper the *Neue Freie Presse* warned him that he was on the verge of being fired and urged him to curtail his absences.

For months, Herzl had sought an audience with the German kaiser Wilhelm II to discuss Zionism, and now he learned that the kaiser was planning a religious pilgrimage to Jerusalem in October as part of a wider trip to the region. Herzl hoped to find a way to circumvent the sultan's continuing opposition to creating any kind of Jewish state-within-a-state in Palestine by getting the kaiser's backing for the creation of a protectorate for the Jews inside Palestine. Herzl wanted the kaiser and Germany to assume protection for the Jews in Palestine, a plan to which he hoped the sultan would not object. In a meeting with one of the kaiser's ambassadors where he first raised the idea, Herzl had been told that the kaiser might be receptive to raising the plan when he met with the sultan. In any event, it was clear to Herzl that it was "the Kaiser's wish to receive a Zionist deputation in Jerusalem," and Herzl now felt he had little choice but to go to the Middle East.

Herzl was then thirty-eight years old, unhappily married and the father of three children, two girls and a boy. His wife, Julia, whose dowry had helped finance his political activities, had no interest in the Zionist movement, the possibility of the founding of a Jewish state, or visiting Palestine. The morning before Herzl's departure, she asked him to bring her back a pair of Ottoman slippers, a popular accessory among the fashionable set in Europe that year. She had insisted that Joseph Seidener, an engineer and fellow Zionist who would accompany Herzl to Jerusalem, get on the floor in the Herzl living room and trace an outline of her foot onto a piece of paper to facilitate the search.

Herzl worried about making the trip because of rumors circulating in Jerusalem, and passed on to him in letters from his supporters, that the sultan, Abdul Hamid II, did not approve of his impending visit or his declarations at Basel that the Zionist movement was seeking the creation of a Jewish state in Palestine. There was even talk that the sultan might have Herzl assassinated or jailed if he appeared in the city. Herzl took the threats seriously. It was said that one of the leaders of the Ottoman army had sent back a bag full of ears he had cut off dead enemy soldiers in order to impress the ruler. The sultan himself was well known for getting rid of his foes, both real and perceived, in a wide variety of clever ways. He had exiled some political agitators to remote corners of the empire, given ostensible promotions to critics that took them far away from Constantinople, and eliminated other nuisances through poisonings, kidnappings, and staged brawls. Other rivals and opponents had simply been locked up in jail with no explanation, or been placed under house arrest for decades.

It was David Wolffsohn, who along with Moses Schnirer, Joseph Seidener, and the German businessman Max Bodenheimer accompanied Herzl to Jerusalem, who came up with the scheme to speak in code during the visit as a way of avoiding a similar fate. The four men agreed that Herzl's code name would be his Hebrew name, Benjamin. They referred to the sultan as "Cohn"—giving him a Jewish-sounding surname as a sly joke. Palestine became "the printing office." They even deemed it too risky to say aloud the name of Herzl's book, *The Jewish State*, referring to it in public only by its initials, "J.S."

To reach Jerusalem they had taken a train from Vienna to Constantinople, then boarded a ship at the port that took them to Alexandria, Smyrna, and even a stop at the Acropolis. Although they feasted on caviar, potato dumplings, and chicken Kiev during the crossing, the boat was packed, and the oppressive heat and choppy waters made it unbearable belowdecks. On the way from Alexandria to the port in Jaffa, the four men slept for two nights in the open air, stretched out on the deck using their cloth bags as pillows. All around them, others were doing the same, and the passengers often spent the long hours talking and sharing stories about their journeys.

In his diary, Herzl described the different groups of people that he met on board, marveling how they all found themselves headed to Palestine from various points in the world. A Russian musician who had only enough money to pay for steerage class constantly complained about the smell of so many unwashed people crowded together. An elderly priest from South Africa was going to Jerusalem to visit Christian holy sites. A group of Arabs who had been working in

Constantinople were headed home with the money they had earned. A poor Jewish woman from Romania whose daughter was sick and living in Jerusalem worried about getting to see her because she had left home hurriedly and did not have a visa in order.

Sitting on deck, watching Palestine's coast grow steadily closer, the heavy scent of Jaffa's famed orange trees permeating the air, Herzl was moved by his first sight of what he called "the Jewish shore" as the boat entered the port. "It is strange what emotions this desolate country stirs up," he conceded in one of his diary entries.

The five men's first stop was Rishon LeZion, one of the oldest Jewish settlements in Palestine, founded in 1882 by members of the Hovevei Zion, or Lovers of Zion, a group from Russia. The beginning of the modern Zionist movement dates to this time. By 1898 the settlers there had already set up the country's first Hebrew school. At Rishon LeZion, Herzl was greeted as a hero by the nearly six hundred people living in the community. Unable to speak any Hebrew, he delivered a speech in German, while one of the villagers stood next to him and translated as he spoke.

Herzl was everywhere greeted as a kind of prophet. Children lined up at the village gates to sing to him, dressed in white, freshly laundered linen and bearing gifts of chocolate. Old men rushed to his side clutching bread and salt, a traditional gesture of hospitality. Groups of farmers left their fields and rode out to meet him on horseback, cheering him on and shooting their rifles in the air as he approached.

During an appearance at one Jewish settlement, three elderly men trailed behind him as he walked, falling to their knees to kiss the tracks he left in the sand. That incident so unsettled Herzl that afterward he made certain never to be seen riding a white donkey while in the country, for fear that people would think he considered himself the Messiah and turn him in to the Ottoman authorities.

With so many settlements to visit, Herzl didn't reach Jerusalem until a week after his arrival, pulling into its train station on a Saturday night after a four-hour ride from Jaffa. The train was overcrowded and moved slowly up the hills to the city because so many people were hanging out the windows, hoping for a breath of air. Herzl himself started to feel feverish and nauseated. It was already late at night when they finally debarked, but they found Jerusalem lit up and as lively as if it were the middle of the day, a full moon giving the city a spectral glow. Couples and friends strolled arm in arm down the streets or sat at small tables drinking and eating at the many crowded, bustling outdoor cafés. They sang along as the Turkish military band presented its regular Saturday night performance of off-key but spirited marching tunes and folk songs in the city square.

"In spite of my weariness," Herzl wrote about his first vision of the city, "Jerusalem and its grand moonlit contours made a deep impression on me. The silhouette of the fortress of Zion, the citadel of David—magnificent! The streets were alive with Jews sauntering in the moonlight."

He barely had the energy to take it all in, let alone to saunter. Because Wolffsohn refused to ride in a carriage to the hotel—the Sabbath had already started, and observant Jews do not ride—they were obliged to walk from the train station to the hotel, a two-mile journey through mainly unpaved streets. Herzl's gait was unsteady, and he tottered most of the way, held up between the arms of Wolffsohn and the uncomplaining Seidener. When they reached the hotel, they found it crowded with Prussian soldiers who had flooded into Jerusalem as part of the kaiser's entourage. Herzl sat outside on the steps, exhausted, while his friends negotiated for a room for the night.

Herzl's favorite bedtime ritual at home was drinking a bottle of Bavarian beer to help him fall asleep, but Schnirer made him down a glass of camphor oil that night in the hope it would cure his ills (it made Herzl vomit). The doctor then spent the night on the hotel room floor stretched out uncomfortably next to Herzl's bed, ready to help in case he took a turn for the worse. But by the next day Herzl's energy had returned, and he insisted upon exploring the city.

Like many first-time visitors to Jerusalem, the group decided to see the Wailing Wall. The massive structure, which girded the area where the Jewish Temple stood until its destruction by the Roman army in 70 AD, had come to symbolize Jewish longing for the city. Jews from all over the world traveled to Jerusalem to pray there, where every day they stood, their heads pressed against the wall's huge oblong stones, thrusting small, tightly wadded pieces of paper with prayers written on them into the rocks' crevices.

But this warm October morning, Herzl had not come to pray. For him, the Wailing Wall was not a place to ask God for favors, and he did not in any case consider himself a particularly religious man. Joining the morning crowd that thronged the Old City, his group entered at the Jaffa Gate, the main entrance to the bazaar whose narrow alleyways led to the wall. Their route took them past the police station, whose officers were dressed in uniforms that boasted gold buttons and a long, curved scimitar jammed into a leather belt. From a tall tree right outside the gate, criminals' bodies often swung for days after public hangings. As Herzl walked down the main alley that led to the Wailing Wall, vendors and shopkeepers were setting out their wares, while small groups of men sat clustered tightly together around oblong tables at the cafés, sipping tiny cups of black coffee. Bags of chickpeas and barley, salted nuts and dried fruit were stacked up outside the stores, and on one street corner a man plucked chickens and then set them to roast as customers waited. The smell of the cooking meat blended in with the aromas from a kebab restaurant, where slabs of lamb turned on a spit from the early hours of the morning. There were small juice stands where a young boy was always available to squeeze oranges, lemons, or pomegranates, as well as vendors selling sweets, pink, white, yellow, and orange confections in all sizes and shapes, piled in neatly arranged stacks. At local bakeries, fresh rolls twisted in the shape of a wheel and sprinkled with sesame seeds came out of the ovens tray after tray.

Despite the hum of activity all around him, Herzl, who had filled eighteen thick notebooks chronicling his six-year effort to found a Jewish state, was not impressed by anything he saw that day. "When I remember thee in days to come, O Jerusalem," he wrote, soon after arriving in the city, "it will not be with delight."

Herzl's complaints about Jerusalem ranged widely. He found it dirty and dingy, its alleys reeking of dung and garbage. Everything smelled strange to him, from the pungent odors of turmeric, curry, and other spices spilling from burlap sacks sliced open at the top, to the strong scent of donkey sweat as the animals transported people and packages up and down the stone pathways that led into the center of town. "If Jerusalem is ever ours," he wrote in one entry, "and if I were still able to do anything about it, I would begin by cleaning it up." He himself loved to take long, leisurely baths, where he did some of his best thinking, and often practiced his speeches or read drafts of his latest articles aloud while he sat soaking.

Jerusalem was set atop a line of rolling hills. The city's buildings, constructed of stones taken from the same quarries that had been used by builders since the time of the Jewish Temple, remained cool during the day. But outdoors the heat at midday could be stifling, especially for an ailing European who insisted on dressing as if he were back home in Vienna. Herzl filled his diaries with descriptions of the various outfits he wore to meet the dignitaries, notables, and wealthy patrons whom he was trying to persuade to support the Zionist cause. Today, on his way to the Wailing Wall, he refused to take off his jacket, even at the height of the day's heat. To protect himself against the sun, he wore an oversized white hat with a net hanging down over the front. He was impossible to miss.

By then, his elegant face, with its high cheekbones, aquiline nose, and full beard, had adorned so many Zionist posters and flags, appeared in so many articles and handbills, that everyone seemed to recognize him, even some of the beggars who congregated near the wall in the hope of winning a few coins from a generous visitor. Not everyone welcomed his presence, though. Many of Jerusalem's leading civic figures and prominent rabbis did not invite him to their homes or show any interest in meeting him during his visit.

When a huge celebration was held in a tent at the center of the city to celebrate the kaiser's arrival, Herzl had to watch it from his hotel room, almost as if he were in exile, because the Jewish community leaders pointedly refused to include him in the day's festivities. They did not want to compromise their own positions with the Ottoman authorities by appearing to be too closely tied to the Zionist leader.

As Herzl and his companions made their way through the market, they passed other sites of pilgrimage located near the Wailing Wall, such as the Church of the Holy Sepulchre, where the Christian faithful waited for hours for a chance to kiss the tomb from which the body of Jesus had supposedly risen. Herzl insisted on stopping for a moment to observe the crowd, despite protests from his friends, who feared that the presence of Jews would anger those who were impatiently lined up outside. As they got closer to the wall, they could see the shadow of the magnificent Dome of the Rock looming over the city. Underneath its golden cupola, refurbished by Jewish craftsmen in honor of the kaiser's visit to Jerusalem, was the huge rock where the Bible said Abraham went to sacrifice Isaac, and from where Muhammad took his last step on earth, according to Muslim tradition. Jews called the area the Temple Mount, because the Jewish temple had once stood on the site, while Muslims referred to it as the Haram al-Sharif, or Noble Sanctuary.

When they finally pushed their way through the crowds, Herzl stood for a few moments in front of the wall, his hands reverently touching the sacred stones. But the experience was a disappointment, and he reported that he felt nothing. "Any deep emotion is rendered impossible by the hideous, miserable scrambling beggary pervading the place," he wrote in his journal. Recalling the walk past the excited pilgrims, he added, "What superstition and fanaticism on every side!"

The group made their way back through the bazaar and then decided to explore the rest of the city. This time, they headed for the Jerusalem of the future, walking through some of the new neighborhoods that had sprung up in recent years outside the Old City's walls. During their stroll, Herzl pointed out to his friends the sight of three burly porters heading down the street bearing heavy loads strapped to their backs. Dressed in loose caftans that fell to their thighs and were cinched by wide cloth belts, and with dark skin the color of walnuts, the porters looked nothing like the men Herzl knew back at home. He was shocked to learn that the three were Jews and quickly told Wolffsohn to take a picture. They handed the men a few coins and asked them to look into the camera's lens. The porters linked their arms loosely around one another's waists, expressions of bemusement on their faces. Herzl, who never let his misgivings get in the way of his enthusiasm, felt his mood lifting. "If we can bring here 300,000 Jews like this," he declared enthusiastically to his friends, "all of the Land of Israel will be ours."

Although Kaiser Wilhelm II had insisted that Herzl come to Jerusalem, days passed as his aides refused to set a time for their meeting. When the ship that Herzl intended to leave on set sail, he grew increasingly anxious that he would never get the chance to present his ideas to the German leader.

He tried to keep busy by working on his address, and anxiously checked the clothing that he wanted the men to wear once they were finally granted an audience. Laying it all out on his bed, he decided that Bodenheimer's silk top hat needed replacing, and sent him off to the market to try to find one, and a new tie as well.

To pass the time, the men also decided to put together a small gift for the kaiser, a collection of photos of the Jewish settlements that would vividly illustrate the possibilities offered by nascent Jewish nationalism in Palestine. They chose a beautiful calfskin leather album that they found in a small shop in downtown Jerusalem. Its cover was smooth to the touch, and its cream-colored pages were an ideal background to show off the photographs. While they were assembling it, a message arrived summoning Herzl and his group to the kaiser's encampment, a veritable city within the city.

The kaiser's huge entourage had set up thirty billowing white tents on top of an incline directly before the entrance to Jerusalem, the very spot where the Bible said the Babylonians encamped before charging into and sacking the city, exiling the Jews from the land of Israel. It was also the site where the Romans camped before they destroyed the Temple and sent the Jews into another exile. Now Herzl was proposing to reverse the process.

The four men quickly dressed in their freshly pressed black formal wear, top hats, bow ties, and white gloves. Herzl would not let them eat anything before the meeting; he wanted everyone to be in fighting form. When Dr. Schnirer suggested that they drink bromide to calm their nerves, Herzl refused, and insisted that the others abstain as well. He wanted nothing to go wrong.

When they reached the kaiser's encampment, they had their picture taken—five men in formal dress, posed against the skyline of Jerusalem. Standing at the side of the photo is the Arab peasant who drove their carriage, his white turban and long loose gown providing a stark contrast to the stiff bearing of Herzl and his companions. He has an expression of disbelief on his face as the men stand with sand swirling at their feet to record the historic moment.

Before they were allowed to meet the kaiser, Herzl's address was handed back to him, annotated by a functionary in the leader's office. Every reference to a Jewish state in Palestine or the possibility of one's existing someday in the future had been excised, as had any mention of the Zionist congresses, Jewish national aspirations, a Jewish revival, or the Jewish people's ancient connection to the land. "I inferred that our stock had somewhat depreciated," Herzl noted wryly in his journal.

Still, he was undaunted; they had come too far to leave without a meeting. The group was led through the warren of tents to the largest one on the hill. Inside, huge rugs were laid out on the ground and piled high with pillows. The kaiser himself greeted them with a riding whip gripped firmly in his right hand, which he smacked against his palm as he spoke.

The kaiser kept the ensuing conversation polite, informal, and brief. Palestine was a land that needed men, Herzl explained, and he had men who desperately needed a land. The two then talked about the heat, which even in October had often been over 100 degrees. The kaiser reiterated that a hot country like Palestine would need huge sources of water, an observation with which Herzl politely agreed. The session was over quickly, and Herzl summarized it in a single sentence: "He said neither yes nor no."

But even then, Herzl realized that he had failed. Later, his father reported to him that a small news item had appeared in the newspapers about the meeting in Jerusalem. It said that a delegation from the Zionist movement had presented the kaiser with a photo album of pictures of Jewish colonists in Palestine. No mention was made of any political discussion. The trip to Jerusalem had been another dead end.

Getting out of Palestine was no easy task. Herzl packed as soon as he returned to the hotel, and the group left Jerusalem by early-morning train for Jaffa, where they hoped to find a ship willing to take them to Egypt and then on to Europe. Only one ship was considered sturdy enough for travel, and it left on Tuesdays. Herzl spent that Thursday unsuccessfully trying to convince someone with a private yacht to sail him and his friends out of the city.

Finally, early on Friday morning, the group rowed out to a British ship that was transporting crated oranges out of the port, and its captain agreed to let them board. Their cabins were next to the boiler room and got so hot that they were uninhabitable. The men spent the entire time on deck, where everyone got seasick except Herzl.

2

From the vantage of a hilltop, Jerusalem in 1898 looked much the same as it had been described in the Bible. Its hills were dotted with cypress trees, shepherds still guided their flocks over the rocky terraces, and women carried water from wells in jugs balanced on top of their heads. As in ancient times, the ochre stone of the buildings turned to pink in the fading light. The purple and mauve mountains of Moab could be seen over the horizon in the distance, and at the corner of one's eye, the first hint of the Dead Sea's austere shoreline. It was hard not to be moved by such transcendent beauty.

Within its precincts, the city still remained parochial in many ways. There were no phones, only telegraph machines, which were strictly monitored by the Ottoman officials, who kept copies of all outgoing messages. Epidemics of cholera were frequent because of the inadequate hygiene and growing population living in close quarters. A train ran from Jaffa to Jerusalem, but it took so long that many people still preferred to travel by horseback.

In the narrow cobbled streets of the Old City, small boys drove donkeys forward with slaps on their haunches. Greek priests, bearded

and robed, walked balancing hats that looked like black towers trembling atop their heads. Religious leaders sat atop leopardskin thrones
and greeted followers in dank, cramped alcoves, dispensing blessings
and advice and collecting alms for the poor. Herzl found himself in a
crowd that included Arab men in long white robes, Jews from Yemen
with long sidelocks, Russians in caftans and caps, Turks in red fezzes
and frock coats. Even amid the din of the populace, a steady clicking
sound could be heard throughout the day as bodyguards, dressed in
magenta pantaloons, shiny scimitars jutting from the side of thick
belts, struck the cobblestones with silver-headed staffs, warning pe-
destrians to give way. These colorful guards were assigned to anyone
of importance or interest in the city in order both to protect them
and to spy on them.

Although accurate population figures for this time are difficult to
ascertain, by 1896—two years before Herzl's visit—Jews constituted
the majority in Jerusalem. An estimated 28,110 Jews, 8,750 Christians, and 8,560 Muslims lived in the city. Muslims dominated political life, though, because they comprised the majority of Jerusalem's
inhabitants that held Ottoman citizenship, which gave them the
right to vote. Many of the Jews and Christians chose to retain foreign passports and did not become Ottoman citizens.

By the time of Herzl's visit, Jerusalem was the largest and most
politically important city in Palestine, as well as a bustling commercial center for goods that were sent to its market from all over the
area: sweet oranges from Jaffa, heavy robes from Bethlehem, coal
from Hebron to keep homes warm through the winter. As transpor-
tation from Europe to Palestine improved, tourism also became a
lucrative source of steady income, with growing numbers of people
eager to visit Jerusalem streaming into the city.

A religious revival in Europe during this period had resulted in a
newfound interest in the biblical lands. Various European powers,
including Britain and Germany, set up archaeological and scientific

societies in Jerusalem, and sponsored digs all over Palestine searching for the sites of the biblical stories. Clerics of various religions and their followers came to Jerusalem eager to spread their beliefs and live in the place that was such a crucial part of their faith. Austria, France, Russia, and other countries, hoping to increase their political presence in Jerusalem, established their own post offices, promising rapid mail delivery to points all over Europe.

A series of reforms that had been launched in the period from 1839 to 1876, known as the Tanzimat, had simultaneously set in motion forces that the Ottomans found increasingly difficult to control. Laws were passed granting every religion equal status. Christians openly preached and began conversion campaigns. All citizens were now allowed to purchase land, as were foreigners, and Jews began to buy property in Palestine to set up new settlements. In response to these developments, the Ottoman government tried to strengthen its hold on Jerusalem. In 1887, the city was declared a separate municipal entity for the first time since coming under Ottoman rule more than three hundred years earlier. This meant that the city's officials were now directly responsible to the sultan in Constantinople.

By 1898 the Ottomans had become increasingly preoccupied with merely trying to keep their sprawling empire together. Large ethnic groups under their authority were demanding greater autonomy. There were skirmishes with Ottoman soldiers in cities close to the borders of Constantinople. The Ottomans began focusing most of their attention on the Balkans and other regions, leaving Jerusalem for the most part to run its own affairs.

Prominent local Arabs accordingly seized the initiative. Families like the Husseinis and Khalidis, who could often trace their ancestry back to the Prophet Muhammad or an individual close to him, became mediators with the central government on behalf of the people. They gained control of the lucrative appointments to religious offices, which gave them the right to administer the lands owned by mosques. As the nominal protectors of the villagers, they used their position to acquire large landholdings, further consolidating their power base. They sent their sons to the best schools in the empire to acquire foreign languages, diplomatic skills, and well-positioned patrons that would enable them to win appointments in the bureaucracy. Most important, the leading Arab families served as religious leaders in the mosques, keepers of the Dome of the Rock, guardians of the Noble Sanctuary complex, and tax collectors—the key positions of power in Jerusalem. The Khalidi family, one of three that held the keys to the Holy Sepulchre, was responsible for locking it every night to ensure that the various Christian sects that worshipped there did not argue over the space.

Even before Herzl's visit, these Arab families had been urging the sultan to start restricting Jewish immigration to Palestine. In 1891, five hundred representatives of the leading Arab families signed a petition asking the sultan to stop Jews from purchasing land there. Efforts were consequently made to better control Jewish entry into the country. Visitors were required to turn over their passports in exchange for "red cards" that were valid for only a few months. Some of the laws passed during the Tanzimat period were rolled back, and only Ottoman citizens were now allowed to buy land. But there were always ways around these restrictions. Many Jewish immigrants paid bribes so they did not have to turn over their passports. Zionist groups that wanted to purchase property made private arrangements with Ottoman Jewish citizens, who were still able to do so.

There had always been some degree of tension between the different groups that inhabited Jerusalem. Various Christian sects fought with one another for control over the Holy Sepulchre. Riots between Christians, Jews, and Muslims occasionally broke out, especially during holidays, when the city overflowed with people from the villages who traveled to Jerusalem to celebrate and pray.

But in many ways, Herzl's visit in 1898 marked a kind of turning point. For all its problems, Ottoman control had been responsible for the longest peaceful period Jerusalem had known. Now the rise of nationalism was shrinking the shared traditions and communal space that had always been a central part of the fabric of life in the city.

There was a long-standing custom in Jerusalem that two boys born on the same day and in the same neighborhood were each suckled by both mothers, and were then considered foster brothers. Families of the boys often celebrated the children's birthdays together and visited each other's homes during holidays. Everyone set his watch to the same clock, which sat on a large stone base at the entrance to the Old City. Virtually all men wore a beard or a mustache. A man never went out of the house without his magenta fez, and it was said that a true Jerusalemite could tell by the tip of someone's hat if he was amenable to making a loan, doing a favor, or entertaining a business proposition. There were stores in the Old City where one could get the hat blocked, and their owners sat chatting idly as the workers steamed the tops of the hats flat and smooth again. Everyone could tell who was rich and who was poor by counting the number of lanterns their servants carried in the evenings, lighting the way along the dark streets as their employers made their way along unpaved, unlit roads to spend the evening at homes of friends, talking far into the night.

On sunny days and special holidays, Jerusalem families packed a meal and rode out to the tomb of Nebi Samuel for picnics, spreading blankets on the ground outside the tomb and spending the entire day there. Twice a year, Jews, Muslims, and Christians celebrated together at the shrine of Simon the Just, a popular biblical figure. For a single coin you could buy a ride to the tombs on a camel or donkey. Their owners would lead the animals from café to café soliciting business, the colored rocks worn around the beasts' necks to protect them from the evil eye clicking rhythmically as they made their way down the street. During the monthlong Muslim holiday of Ramadan, night-time shows featured entertainers who would make shadow puppets against the walls of a café, often using the puppets' dialogue to poke fun at local officials or make veiled political commentary on the latest events. During the Jewish holiday of Purim, children from all over the city dressed up in colorful costumes to celebrate and exchange sweets. The Arabs even had a name for Purim in their own language, which translated as "the sugar holiday."

The city had its own rhythms, a music that wound its way through everyone's lives. People walked home from work to the sound of Arab melodies played by musicians in the cafés. In the evenings, after dinner was over and the humid air started to give way to cooler breezes, families would stroll over to one of the cafés near the entrance to the main gate of the Old City, where they could listen to a singer perform and catch up on the latest gossip.

These shared experiences set the pace of life in the city and gave Jerusalem its unique flavor. Everyone knew that you could buy hot, freshly baked rolls each morning and afternoon by the main gate. The boys who sold them would include a pinch of zatar, a tasty spice, wrapped tightly inside a wad of old newspaper, into which chunks of bread could be dipped. Wandering through the Old City, one could find a rabbi, imam, or priest taking turns spending part of each day sitting in one of the neighborhood's many shops, available to talk to anyone who stopped in with a problem or needed some advice. Shopkeepers jockeyed for a chance to host one of the religious leaders in their stores, believing it brought good fortune, blessings, and more customers.

Muslims and Jews were business partners in the various markets of the Old City. They lived in the same buildings; often Jews rented their homes from Muslim owners. When a Muslim pilgrim went to Mecca, Jewish neighbors came to visit upon his return to offer their congratulations. Families from different religions made loans to one another, or vouched for one another at the bank. Jews brought their copper pans to the market to be thoroughly steamed and cleaned by Muslim shop owners before the Passover holiday in the spring. People often got their news together—in flyers pasted up on the walls and gates of the city, or at "reading nights" held periodically in the most popular cafés.

3

In 1898 Jerusalem's mayor was Yusuf Khalidi, a member of the prominent Arab family. Although he and Herzl never met during Herzl's visit, it is likely they crossed paths at the many celebrations honoring the kaiser throughout the city.

Khalidi had followed Herzl's career closely. He had read *The Jewish State*, and urged his nephew, Ruhi Khalidi, to read it, too. He did not dismiss the Zionist vision or consider Herzl a madman. Jerusalem was, after all, a city filled with people with messianic visions, and Herzl was, in Khalidi's words, a "Jewish patriot."

Later, months after Herzl had left Jerusalem and returned to Vienna, Khalidi sent a letter to his acquaintance the chief rabbi of Paris, who had ties to Herzl and other Zionist leaders. In it he expressed his hope that Herzl could be persuaded to find another place besides Palestine in which to settle Jews; the rabbi passed the letter along to Herzl and asked him to respond directly to Khalidi, who had written, "The destiny of nations is governed not by abstract concepts, however pure and noble they may be. One must consider reality and respect established facts, the force, yes, the brutal force, of circumstance. The reality is that Palestine is now an integral part of the Ottoman Empire, and what is more serious, it is inhabited by others than Israelites."

Herzl replied to Khalidi on March 19, 1899: "As you yourself said, there is no military power behind the Jews. As a people, they have long lost the taste for war, they are a thoroughly pacific element, and fully content if left in peace. Therefore there is absolutely no reason to fear their immigration."

Herzl went on to try to reassure Khalidi that Muslims and Christians would benefit from Zionism: "Do you believe that an Arab who owns land in Palestine, or a house worth three or four thousand francs, will be sorry to see their value rise five- and ten-fold? But this would most certainly happen with the coming of the Jews. And this is what one must bring the natives to comprehend . . . if one looks at the matter from this viewpoint, and it is the right viewpoint, one inevitably becomes a friend of Zionism."

As soon as Herzl returned home from his trip to Palestine, he started work on another book, the futuristic novel *Old-New Land*, in which he tried to transform his disappointment in Jerusalem into an imaginative vision of his dream for Palestine in the future. *Old-New Land* wasn't a success with the general reading public when it appeared in 1902, but it was a vivid depiction of key Zionist themes and aspirations. Set in Palestine in 1923, it is told through the eyes of a man who, like Herzl, had last visited Palestine in 1898. When he returns twenty-five years later, it has undergone a remarkable transformation. The Jews have taken over the country and established a system of government called the New Society, which individuals of any religious background could join and enjoy full rights of participation.

The novel even features a character called Reschid Bey, supposedly modeled after Yusuf Khalidi, who is described as a Muslim dressed in dark European clothing and a red fez. In the book, Reschid is asked how the "former inhabitants [of Palestine] fared—those who had nothing, the numerous Moslem Arabs." Reschid responds with an argument very similar to the one Herzl had made in his letter to Yusuf Khalidi: namely, that Muslims would gain opportunities to work and a newfound prosperity from the influx of Jewish immigration and the establishment of the New Society in Palestine. "Nothing could have been more wretched than an Arab village at the end of the nineteenth century. . . . Now everything is different. . . . When the swamps were drained, the canals built, and the eucalyptus trees planted to drain, and cure the marshy soil, the natives (who, naturally, were well acclimatized) were the first to be employed and were paid well for their work," Reschid rhapsodizes.

When Reschid is asked if, despite the improvements they introduced, he regards the Jews as intruders, he replies, "Would you call a man a robber who takes nothing from you, but brings you something instead? The Jews have enriched us. Why should we be angry with them? They dwell among us like brothers. Why should we not love them?"

Yusuf Khalidi never became a friend of Zionism, nor did his nephew Ruhi, who in subsequent years became one of its most high-profile critics. Ruhi Khalidi had made a concerted effort to better understand Zionist culture. When he was in Constantinople, he attended plays produced by a Yiddish theater company that dramatized how pogroms in Russia had led to so many Jews leaving the country in search of other places to live, including Palestine. He briefly studied, though never formally enrolled, at the Alliance Israelite school in Jerusalem, a Jewish, albeit non-Zionist, institution that taught French, Hebrew, and other subjects. He may have picked up some Hebrew; among his books and papers were Hebrew-language textbooks, and an Arabic-Hebrew, Russian-Hebrew, and French-Hebrew dictionary. In one of the journals that Ruhi Khalidi kept, he wrote out the words to "Hatikvah," the song popularized by Zionist groups describing the Jewish longing to return to Jerusalem, which later became the anthem of the state of Israel.

Ruhi Khalidi especially struggled to understand why Herzl, who had seemed in pages of *The Jewish State* willing to consider other sites for the Jewish homeland, was now insistent on Palestine alone. In fact, at the Zionist Congress of 1902, Herzl did raise the issue of discussing alternate sites for the future Jewish homeland, as a purely practical matter. Pogroms in Russia had been growing increasingly violent, and anti-Semitism threatened Jews all over Europe. Time did not appear to be on Herzl's side. The sultan, meanwhile, had made it clear in several meetings with Herzl that he was no closer to agreeing to the idea of a Jewish national presence in Palestine than he had ever been. The Jews were welcome in the Ottoman Empire, he had reiterated to Herzl, but only if they agreed to settle in groups of no more than 250 people and in places other than Palestine. He also insisted that they relinquish their foreign passports and become Ottoman citizens.

Then the British came forward with a proposal to establish a Jewish colony in a portion of East Africa they controlled. Herzl thought it might be an idea worth pursuing, for while East Africa was not Palestine, he believed that it offered the only immediate solution to finding a safe place for persecuted Jews to move. He saw the proposal as a temporary haven, until circumstances changed in Palestine.

But he was taken aback at the reaction of the Zionist Congress to his suggestion that a small group be organized to study the possibility. Delegates jumped on their chairs and booed, clenched fists raised in the air. Many threatened to leave and abandon the movement. Victor Jacobson, who would later set up the Zionist offices in Constantinople after the Young Turks came to power in 1908, told the Congress that disengaging in any way from the idea of a homeland in Palestine would result in irreparable damage to their cause. At one point, he stormed out of the meeting hall, part of a massive walkout with others who joined him in protest.

The incident so rattled Herzl that at the conclusion of the Congress he stood, raised his right hand, and intoned the famous biblical passage: "If I forget thee, O Jerusalem, let my right hand forget her cunning."

Ruhi Khalidi eventually concluded that Herzl had seen that he had had no other choice but to make a pragmatic accommodation to the most militant faction of Zionists. Khalidi believed that Herzl was fundamentally a pragmatist, and it was that conviction that gave him hope that violence in Palestine could be averted. Both Ruhi and Yusuf felt that Herzl and the Zionists would soon realize that, despite their oath of loyalty to Jerusalem, they were outnumbered. Surely they would acknowledge the inevitable and try to avert disaster?

But by now each side had already made a crucial misjudgment that would continue to affect its policies in Palestine for years to come: the Muslims were convinced the Jews could never win, while the Jews believed the Arabs would someday yield.

4

Albert Antebi, born in Damascus, arrived in Jerusalem in 1896 to serve as the assistant to the head of the Alliance Israelite school. Through the force of his strong personality, his ability to read faces, and his exquisite sensitivity to the various traditions of Ottoman culture, he quickly amassed enormous power in Jerusalem and came to know everyone of prominence in the city. Long before Herzl worried about being seen riding on a white donkey in Jerusalem, Antebi was familiarly known as "King of the Jews," though his nicknames varied. Some called him "Little Herod," after the last Jewish ruler in Jerusalem before the destruction of the Second Temple, because he wielded enormous power in the governor's quarters, and was willing to use it to oppose those with whom he disagreed. Many considered him a despot, whose tyrannical behavior was unpredictable. Others referred to him as the "Jewish Pasha," in tribute to his effective lobbying on behalf of the Jewish community.

He had friends everywhere. He maintained cordial relations with Yusuf Khalidi, whom he would meet from time to time at the governor's house, where everyone with a little influence in the city came to press his case for money, attention, or redress with the Ottoman government's representative in town. He clashed with Ruhi Khalidi because he resented the younger man's aggressive efforts to restrict Jewish immigration to Palestine and oppose land sales to Jews, even Jews like the Antebis, who had been Ottoman citizens for centuries.

Antebi had grown up in a religious family, where in each generation one of the men invariably chose to become a rabbi. Despite his penchant for drinking (he had acquired a taste for champagne while studying in Paris, where he went in 1880 at the age of eleven to complete his formal education), smoking, gambling, and flirtations, Antebi considered himself a traditional Jew. He and his wife had seven children and kept a kosher home. They prayed together at the local synagogue every Friday night and Saturday and did not ride on the Sabbath. Antebi was a generous contributor to all causes in Jerusalem, both inside and outside the Jewish community. But he did not approve of the fact that so many Jews in Jerusalem were surviving on charitable donations from abroad and argued passionately for Jewish economic independence.

This belief should have placed him comfortably on the side of the Zionists, but as it happened, he intensely disliked Herzl. The two men met only once, during Herzl's visit to Jerusalem, at one of the many cocktail parties hosted in the city to celebrate the kaiser's visit. Antebi's antipathy toward Herzl was deep and somewhat surprising, since they shared many qualities, not the least of which was charm. At one party, Herzl had been asked by a well-dressed woman about the rationale for having a Jewish state. He had gallantly replied, "The glamour of your company in Jerusalem would increase our enjoyment of life considerably."

Like Herzl, Antebi had been politically awakened by a famous case of anti-Semitism. In 1840, twenty-nine years before he was born, Antebi's grandfather, Jacob Antebi, the chief rabbi of Damascus, was arrested and falsely accused of being part of a group that had kidnapped two men and murdered them to use their blood to make matzo for Passover. The case, which came to be known as the Damascus blood libel, was as famous in its day as the Dreyfus affair. Eventually, due to international pressure, Antebi and the other prisoners were freed, but not before being tortured.

Albert Antebi never discussed the incident publicly. But he stressed tirelessly the need for Jews to build up economic resources, to develop their own businesses, to contribute to the larger community. He argued that it was critical that Jews forge strong relationships and partnerships with Muslims, rather than live separately. He believed the Jews' continued presence and safety in Jerusalem was dependent on their ability to coexist peacefully with their Muslim neighbors.

Not surprisingly, Antebi increasingly found himself caught in an awkward position between the two rival communities. He was proud that the Alliance Israelite school was chosen to help with the restoration of the Dome of the Rock mosque for the kaiser's visit; the ball at the top of the lead dome was repaired at the school's metal workshop. He bragged about the party he was throwing in his home during the kaiser's trip, and how not only Jewish leaders but the governor's entire harem and the city's key Muslim personalities would be attending. He worked closely in many city business groups with Jamal

Husseini, whose son attended the Alliance Israelite school and became a close childhood friend of one of Antebi's sons. He disliked the way the Zionists loudly proclaimed that they would hire only Jews to work on their settlements, angering Muslim peasants who had toiled on the land for years.

"I want to conquer Zion economically and not politically," Antebi explained in one letter that articulated his opposition to the Zionists. "I want to cherish the historic and spiritual Jerusalem not the modern and temporal one." He concluded, "I want to be a Jewish deputy in the Ottoman Parliament and not in the Hebrew Temple of Moriah."

Although Antebi was reviled for his focus on Jewish economic power by Jerusalem's traditional Jewish community, his ideas were embraced by the Zionists, who saw economic power as a road to political dominance. Antebi soon realized that he had to do business with them, for they alone shared his commitment to strategies like buying land and setting up Jewish schools.

Antebi used his connections in France to become a land broker in Palestine, representing charitable organizations run by some of the wealthiest foreign Jews, including Baron Rothschild, to buy property throughout the country. His network of contacts at the governor's house would inform him of Arab landowners willing to sell, and he spent huge sums to obtain these parcels. He focused on obtaining contiguous plots, recognizing that a stretch of land controlled by Jewish settlers gave them more power than isolated settlements spread all over the country.

When times got economically tough in Jerusalem in the early part of the century, however, and work was difficult to find, Antebi arranged to set up a fund that gave small cash allowances to people who wanted to leave Palestine and move elsewhere. That service, not surprisingly, outraged the Zionists, and articles appeared in the local press denouncing him as a traitor to the cause. But the pragmatic

Antebi felt it made no sense to live in Zion without a means to support a family and buy food.

Antebi had followed the proceedings of the 1905 Zionist Congress held in Basel, the first to be convened following Herzl's death at age forty-four a year earlier. "Never was so much evil done to the Palestinian cause by this unreflective manifestation of supporters of Palestine," Antebi wrote.

The committee that Herzl had authorized at the previous congress to study the question of whether Uganda was a suitable place for Jewish immigration had concluded that it was not, and at the congress the delegates formally voted to reject the idea. The only possible national home for Jews was in Palestine, and the movement's resources should focus there. Antebi had viewed the Uganda commission as a positive development. "It shows to our Ottoman government that Zionism does not exclusively set its sight on Palestine," Antebi wrote.

In Jerusalem, the results of the declaration were immediate and just as Antebi feared: "the strict observation of restrictive measures" limiting the rights of Jews to acquire land in Palestine. The governor of Jerusalem, bowing to the increasing political pressure on him in the wake of the Zionist Congress, opened an official investigation into the recent transfer of lands to Antebi—even though, as Antebi wrote with some resentment, "I am an Ottoman" and should have no problems purchasing land.

When Antebi met with the governor about it, the governor complained about the Zionists' noisy nationalism and its repercussions on all Jews in Palestine. "Your biggest enemies are yourselves," the governor told Antebi.

Instead of focusing on increasing Jewish economic power in Jerusalem by starting businesses with moderate Muslims and Christians, as Antebi pushed, there was debate among the Zionists about whether non-Jewish workers should be given jobs in Jewish settlements. As the Zionists consolidated their power and Muslim resentment in Jerusalem grew, Antebi became increasingly worried about the future. Any notion of a country made up of various peoples united by a common identity seemed to be receding. After a meeting at which he had argued passionately that non-Jewish workers should not be barred from working on Jewish settlements, he wrote in despair to a friend, "Will we prove with our acts that the majority is always intolerant?" In Jerusalem now, "we are but a powerless majority," he wrote. But one day that might change, and the very prospect of success appeared to frighten him most of all. "What would we do," he asked, "if we were given the power?"

PART TWO

Jerusalem 1908

Jerusalem will become Babel . . .

—ALBERT ANTEBI

1

Ali Ekrem, the governor of Jerusalem, quickly made his way through the Old City to his home. It was August 1908, a month after a group of army officers who called themselves the Young Turks had taken over the Ottoman government, forcing the sultan to concede that it was they and not he who now ran the empire. The main celebration of their ascension had just ended, and Ali Ekrem was anxious to write his report and send it to Constantinople while the day's events were still fresh in his mind. Sitting in his private study, where no one was allowed to enter, he wrote in bold letters across the top of a sheet of paper, "Secret." Ekrem wondered why he bothered with that precaution; one of the first things he had learned in Jerusalem was that nothing stayed secret for long.

From the main waiting room Ekrem could hear a steady din of noise. He had divided the house into two sections when he had moved his family to the city two years earlier. Upstairs was the women's area, consisting of the kitchen, the children's bedrooms, and the family's quarters, and no one went there without an invitation. Below were the rooms where Ekrem conducted his own business, receiving guests, listening to news from his informers and spies, drafting official documents.

He started to compose his summary of the day's events: "The voices of happiness of the city of Jerusalem, for which there is no example in all of the world . . . went up to the sky in a thousand languages and styles."

He chronicled the speeches, the handshakes, the festivities. The whole town was decorated in flags, and all over Jerusalem, praise for the elections and freedom could be heard ringing out. "Eyes were blinded from crying," he recorded.

And then he got to the heart of the matter. "My respect and love for my homeland," he complained, "[are] disappearing from the aspersions of two or three rumor-mongers in Jerusalem." This was not just an affront against him, he added with a flourish, but against the "entire nation." Perhaps it would be to his advantage if news of this letter and its contents spread through Jerusalem, Ekrem reflected. He had not been strong enough in combating the people who wanted to see him fail here.

After two years in his post, Ekrem was still struggling with how to fit in among the people of Jerusalem. Back in Constantinople, the spies that trailed him around the city used to come so close to him that he could hear their breathing. But here in Jerusalem, he never felt the breath of his enemies on his neck. Its people were like the city's stones, smooth to the touch but cold, which made it harder to fight back.

Part of Ekrem's disquiet arose from the fact that he had come to Jerusalem to escape. Like his predecessors in the governor's job, at the time of his appointment to Jerusalem he had been serving as the secretary at the palace, a prestigious position that required him to write letters and documents for the sultan and his officials.

Ekrem was used to the vagaries of power. He was the son of Nemak Kemal, a writer and poet honored for his descriptions of the countryside and his paeans to the glorious history of the Ottoman Empire. As beloved as Nemak Kemal had been among the people, however, so had he been hated by the sultan. Throughout Ekrem's childhood, the family moved from town to town because the sultan was always finding a reason to send Nemak Kemal somewhere else—usually to another city farther away from Constantinople. When his father died young, Ekrem was certain it was the constant state of exile and the tension it gave rise to that had killed him.

After his father's death, Ekrem was summoned to the palace. He had been inside the huge complex many times with his father, but it always remained a labyrinth, virtually impossible to navigate. The palace operated as its own city, cut off from the rest of Constantinople, and over the years Ekrem never truly figured out a way to decipher what was happening there. "I was always being suspected," he once told his young daughter, who recorded many of his comments in a diary that she kept of her childhood, "even when honored." He could never completely escape the shadow of suspicion cast by his father's difficult history with the sultan. Ekrem always believed that the real reason the sultan had offered him a place in the palace was to keep a close eye on him.

Even so, he had gotten into trouble. When a close friend of Ekrem's got embroiled in an improper relationship with a member of the sultan's family, Ekrem was pressed into writing letters in his friend's name. His role in the ruse was quickly discovered, and at one point, Ekrem feared the sultan might use his involvement as a pretext for having him killed. He knew that he was in trouble when he was summoned to the palace and an assistant of the sultan explained how Ekrem's presence was urgently needed in Tchataldja, an unimportant city near Constantinople. There was little pay involved, and Tchataldja was so small that it was difficult to locate on a map. Dissatisfied with the assignment, Ekrem spoke to a friend at the palace with connections, who arranged for the current governor of Jerusalem to be posted elsewhere. Ekrem immediately sent a letter to the palace turning down the job in Tchataldja but adding that all his life he had dreamed about going to Jerusalem. The sultan kept him for two hours in the large waiting room before having him ushered in to hear the news that the Jerusalem post was his.

But his stint in Jerusalem had not gone as anticipated. The problems in the city were deeper and more complex than anyone had told him or perhaps even realized. Then just two years after his arrival, the Young Turks had come to power, bringing further change and uncertainty. Ekrem could not decide which group he disliked more—the Jews or the Arabs. Back in Constantinople, those familiar with the machinations of Jerusalem had urged him to court the prominent leaders of each community, and he had been diligent in his attentions to all.

In his first week on the job, he had been required to mediate a dispute between the Greek and Latin patriarchs, who uneasily shared power at the Church of the Holy Sepulchre. The Greek patriarch had apparently provided a new cushion for the seat of the Arab gate-keeper of the Holy Sepulchre. The Latin patriarch came to the gov-ernor's house to register his complaint. If the Greek patriarch was allowed to be the only one to give new cushions, then the granting of the cushions would then become the right of the Greeks. This could upset the delicate balance of power in effect at the church, where to prevent violence among the various factions every ritual had been scrupulously divided between them. Ultimately, after meeting with both sides several times, Ekrem set up a schedule to determine the granting of the cushions: they would be given on certain holidays, and each group would take its turn.

Every time Ekrem tried to accomplish something in Jerusalem, similar disputes arose. When he went one day to visit one of the large villages just outside the city, he faced another potential conflict, because the three largest monasteries there, the Greeks, Catholics, and Armenians, had all invited him and his family to lunch. How could he accept all three invitations? And yet if he chose one over the other, then those who had been turned down would find out, assume he favored one particular side, and violence would ensue.

He decided his only recourse was to eat lunch three times that day. Each of his hosts watched to see what morsels he put in his mouth, how much he consumed, what he drank. He tried scrupulously to eat the same number of courses at each of the three meals and eat neither too much—because then he would lose the ability to keep dining at the other lunches that day—or so little that he might offend any of the groups. He was so self-conscious about each choice and move he made that he barely enjoyed the food that so many people had labored to prepare. His daughter had joked with him afterward that he had managed to avoid a huge fight for the small price of a "glorious stomachache."

He had invited the various heads and family leaders to the governor's house to drink coffee from gold cups, to smoke cheroots, to share their grievances. He had furnished the room where he received guests and conducted business with pieces made by the Alliance Israelite. When positions opened up in the court, or the religious court, or in some other government office, he made sure that a Khalidi or Nashashibi or Husseini got a job.

Somehow, though, the people of Jerusalem never seemed grateful for his solicitousness. They sat as supplicants before him every day, professing all the correct sentiments in the correct order. They affirmed their loyalty: to him, to the sultan, to the empire itself. There was nothing he could fault in any of them, no specific offense of which they were clearly guilty. And while he had always felt that his presence in the city was merely tolerated, Jerusalem's indifference now seemed to be giving way to something else, something more dangerous and threatening.

A few weeks before, he had been given a pamphlet called "Our Program," written by Menachem Ussishkin, one of the leaders of the Zionist movement. Ekrem had met Ussishkin, a burly man with sandy hair and dark eyes, only a few times. He had once encountered him riding on horseback near Jaffa, scouting out land where the Jews wanted to build another new settlement. Ussishkin had given a speech in Hebrew at one of the Zionist congresses, outlining the movement's goals. The speech had been translated into French, and copies had been circulating in Jerusalem. Ussishkin described the situation in Palestine as essentially a competition between the Jews and the Arabs. Victory would go to the side that invested the most money, developed the most skills, built up the most formidable infrastructure. "The Jews have to win," Ussishkin baldly stated.

Ekrem had written a letter to the palace about the document, not even bothering to mark the missive "Secret," hoping that it would get back to the various Jewish groups in Jerusalem that he was well aware of their intentions, that he would not be fooled by their professions of loyalty to the empire. When he wanted to alert the palace to the fact that the attempts to stop Jewish immigration were failing, he ordered the head of the Jaffa port to count the number of Jewish passports that were being held there. Under the new rules, Jewish visitors to Palestine left their passports at the port, trading them for a red identity card that allowed them to travel around the city, and returned within three months to retrieve them when they left Palestine. But in truth, only a few ever left. The rest abandoned their passports and either lived in Jerusalem without one, or used their contacts in the city to obtain another. At last count, 2,372 passports were unclaimed at the port offices, and the number grew every month. Ekrem knew as well as anyone that they would most likely remain there indefinitely, collecting dust.

Ekrem's superiors did not understand why the police were unable to simply track down all of these missing Jews and deport them from the country. When a Jew entered Jerusalem, Ekrem explained, "he has entered his land, his homeland, his home." The police could not find him, because his friends had him in their homes. He would go from house to house, never staying too long in any one place. He did not care if he had no established place, as long as he was able to live in Jerusalem. Sometimes sympathetic officials in one of the various foreign consulates would inform the government that the Jew had died. A few years later, the dead man would miraculously come back to life and get another passport issued. Ekrem had already reduced the amount of time Jews were allowed to stay in Jerusalem as tourists from three months to one. He insisted that a picture of each passport holder be taken for easier identification. He asked for more funding for additional inspectors, more police stations, even for a police boat to patrol the Jaffa harbor and try to prevent people from entering the country without proper documentation. But there was no money to underwrite such measures, and virtually everything Ekrem requested was turned down.

"The Jews in Jerusalem are stronger than any of our estimations," he warned in one letter. He had gone to Rishon LeZion twice, to visit the community that Baron Rothschild had helped found. He had visited the wine cellars, listened to an orchestra from a nearby settlement, and dined with Arthur Ruppin, the head of the group charged with buying land in Palestine. Ruppin headed up the Zionist Organization's Palestine Office and was putting together an effort to purchase arms for every Jewish settlement, for which he had just authorized another 5,000 francs from its funds. His goal was to provide every settlement with from five to twenty rifles. Why did no one in Constantinople see that conflict was brewing?

Ekrem was even more disdainful of the Arabs than he was of the Jews, describing them as insects and dogs. Sometimes he referred to the families that were bothering him in one long word, running "Khalidi-Nashashibi-Husseini" together in a single breath. At other times he identified them simply as "the corrupt"; many of the letters that were dispatched to the palace spoke simply of troubles with "the Jews and the corrupt."

Ekrem had included in a number of his letters reports about new Arab schools, clubs, and social groups. "The declaration of the constitution and its implementation have gradually begun to arouse feelings of independence among the Arabs," he wrote to the minister of the interior shortly after the celebration in Jerusalem. "This idea is at present silent and secret, it is true, but . . . one can feel that the people . . . are tending in this direction." He urged Constantinople to take action against the stirring of nationalism in the city. "It is my opinion that the concept of freedom will lead here to regrettable misuse," he explained. "The corrupt gangs of notables, who regard the ignorant local population as their prey, will regard the idea of freedom as an important means of disobedience and revolt." He went on to suggest that the government choose high-ranking officials in Jerusalem from among fellow Turks, not Arabs. The Arabs were already objecting to the fact that Turkish was the only official language of the state and wanted the right to conduct official correspondence and petitions in Arabic as well. They resented that petitioners in court were required to hire a Turkish translator if they couldn't state their own claims in Turkish rather than in Arabic.

The celebrations in Jerusalem after the ascension of the Young Turks were short-lived. Soon, Ekrem insisted, the Ottomans would have to send more men to the city to keep order if they had any hope of retaining Jerusalem. Unless they found a way to stop the Jews from continuing to flood the city, and the Arabs from continuing to foster their own national culture, there would be only one way to control Jerusalem—"with the help of an army."

2

Albert Antebi pushed his way through the crowd gathered outside the Dome of the Rock mosque. Noon prayers were over, but heaps of shoes, piled up in small pyramids by the penitents who removed them before stepping inside to pray, still remained. Some of the wealthier pilgrims had paid small boys to hold their shoes, but most people had resigned themselves to a long wait digging through all the footwear that was now tossed haphazardly outside the mosque.

There had been reports of men fainting indoors because of the unusual November 1908 heat and the crush of people. The rock was a huge brown boulder with sharp edges that jutted into the air, and the mosque's shape gave visitors the feeling that it had been constructed to make the rock look even more imposing, the golden cupola appearing almost to cradle it. A low gate circumscribed the rock, giving it some protection from the clamoring hands that clawed at it in supplication. Stairs snaked around it, allowing pilgrims to descend into the cavernous darkness below, pressed tightly together, holding on to the rickety handrails, slowly making their way to the bottom on steps that got narrower and narrower. An overpowering clammy smell, of mildew and dampness, left them breathless, their hushed whispers making a tinny echo in the cramped, packed space.

Upstairs, where the main prayers were chanted five times a day, there was scarcely more room, as visitors knelt on the floor in a large crowd. They prayed in a shudder, exhaling as if on cue, as they followed the familiar rituals at an unhurried pace despite the mounting heat. The rugs that covered the mosque's floor were worked in tiny geometric patterns in glimmering, brightly colored threads, which had grown dull from the continual tramping of so many bodies.

It was a Saturday afternoon, a day when the mosque was not usually so crowded. For those who lived far away from Jerusalem, it had been customary to come by horse, by donkey, or, in the past few years, even by train, depending on where one lived, to worship at the Dome of the Rock on Fridays, when the best preachers delivered their sermons, their voices melodious as they called the men to prayer. Although their talks were fiery and infused with passages from the Koran that always seemed relevant to the days' events, the preachers were circumspect in what they actually said, well aware that the mosque was filled with the sultan's spies, eager to report any sedition. Just as the puppeteers who worked the cafés in downtown

Jerusalem put words in their puppets' mouths that they would never have dared say if the lights had been on, so, too, did the preachers find a way to convey to anyone aware of the subtext a message of hope and rebellion.

Inside the mosque on this Saturday the talk was of one thing only, the changes wrought throughout Jerusalem since the revolution by the Young Turks. The first thing the rebels had done was put back into effect the constitution that the sultan had abandoned when he disbanded Parliament back in 1876. They talked about a new approach to running the government, based on the idea that a subject of the empire was an Ottoman first, and then a Muslim, Christian, or Jew. They promised that, under the new regime, everyone would enjoy the same rights. Elections for delegates to the newly formed Parliament had already been held, and the people of Jerusalem had gathered together today to celebrate the change and to hear the speeches by their representatives before they left to take up their positions in Constantinople.

In the courtyard outside the mosque, men sat on the stone benches that were typically used by worshippers to remove their shoes, or sprawled against the sides of the building. Others claimed any available patch of stone or grass along the way to the center of the Old City. Farther from the mosque, families sat together, some with picnics, spreading out blankets and unpacking boiled eggs, cheese, and pita. The children ran from blanket to blanket grabbing food, as they all watched the celebrations and waited to catch sight of the governor, who was expected to give a speech later in the day.

It was difficult to move through so dense a crowd, and Antebi felt constricted in the dark suit that stretched across his expanding middle, the beads of sweat from the midday sun gathering under the rim of his magenta fez. His mustache, which danced on his lip when he smiled, now drooped. He steered clear of the knots of people who gathered around the pairs of men jousting with swords, their cries growing louder each time the blades crashed together. From time to time, the explosive sound of a pistol being fired into the air pierced the din and made him jump in surprise.

Antebi recognized friends in the crowd, and others that he preferred to avoid. Some were neighbors, who had also decided to spend the Sabbath here instead of in the courtyard where the men usually gathered to talk after the afternoon meal, and some acquaintances with whom he played cards late into the evenings after the government offices closed down. Shopkeepers had decided to close early and come to witness the festivities for themselves; clerks in the post offices, government workers, men who offered rides on their donkeys and camels, scholars who spent most of the day inside the mosques and churches and synagogues poring over ancient texts, and porters and bakers and millers—all had taken a break in their daily routine. Some Antebi waved to from across the way. Others he stopped to greet for just a moment, a brief opportunity to press their hands together, or quickly kiss each other's cheeks before the flow of the crowd forced them to part.

As he moved ahead, small boys pressed free boxes of cigarettes into his hands, and someone handed him a glass of lemonade. He felt drops of rosewater fall in a fine mist on his face, dispensed by women sitting on the balconies and rooftops above, who sprayed the scented water on the revelers as a sign of good luck and a turn of fortune. Also in the air was the pungent smell of burning coffee, kept too long in the large kettles that men carried on their backs, offered today gratis to anyone who asked, in small cups. Others threw flower petals onto the steps leading up to the mosque, to make the way to prayer sweet-smelling.

Antebi loved festivities, but today his mind was distracted. Just as the mountains against which Jerusalem sat seemed to shift colors as the sun set, going from a deep purple to pink to a sandstone yellow, so, too, did the moods of the city. Lately, he had been worrying, and he could not help but feel that all the people gathered here today had come to celebrate something that seemed tenuous at best. The Arabs shooting off pistols, the groups of Jewish men carrying a replica of the Ten Commandments with the slogan "fraternity, equality, liberty" written in gold letters on its back, and the people who wore pins in their lapels bearing the same phrase all expected great changes from the elections. Antebi knew that such intense elation, fraught with expectation, could well result in huge disappointment.

"We are the majority [in Jerusalem], but we have no official representative in the municipality, nor in the administrative council, nor in the courts," Antebi wrote to a friend about the situation in the city. Part of that lack of representation was due to the fact that so few Jews became Ottoman citizens and so could not vote. But Jews didn't even receive the same number of invitations as the Christian groups to the governor's formal events, though they vastly outnumbered them in the city.

As Jews purchased more land in Palestine, they were met with increasing outbreaks of violence. Sometimes a confrontation would start in the fields when they tried to till the land they had just bought. But incidents had also been reported in Jaffa, where many of the young Jews and Muslims liked to go and drink after work, their faces to the sea. Representatives of the Zionists' Palestine Office, which had been set up in Jaffa earlier that year, feared that news of the conflicts would discourage other Jews from wanting to immigrate.

Antebi found himself increasingly being called in as a mediator. When a few months earlier the Zionists had held a march celebrating a Jewish holiday and danced through the streets of Jaffa carrying banners, some young Muslim men had taunted them, calling out, "These are the dogs that want to take over our country." Fighting had broken out, and two men had been killed. Antebi had had to pay bribes and call in favors to get some of those involved released from jail. "Is it logical, wise and practical to stir up vanity, to stir up hatred and to throw in the public our pretentious cry: Judea for Judeans of old?" he asked the Zionist leaders.

Despite his reservations about the Zionists, Antebi had found himself working with them more often over the past few months. The Zionists had been caught off guard by the Young Turk revolution and the shift in political power away from the sultan. It had made some of them more amenable to collaborating with Antebi, whose deep roots in the region gave him a wide variety of contacts.

Antebi had responded with enthusiasm, hopeful that the Zionists would embrace his idea of increasing Jewish economic influence in Jerusalem, rather than exclusively focusing on seizing political power. He had attended meetings with them, formed committees, and written memos and letters suggesting creative ways to pool the various groups' money together to create loan funds to encourage Jewish settlers to buy land and found settlements. They had talked about setting up banks, giving aid to schools, and trying to join forces to lobby the government. They were working on establishing a common curriculum for all the Jewish-run schools, including Antebi's Alliance Israelite, even though the Alliance was not formally identified with the Zionist movement. "The Zionists finally realize that they need a union of all the Jewish forces in the country," Antebi had asserted.

But the Zionists proved to be both hasty and impatient, and seldom took the time to listen to people who had lived and worked with the Turks for far longer than they had—such as Antebi. "They think they are dealing with a European country," Antebi once said, frustrated with their always expecting immediate action and a quick reply.

For his own part, Antebi did not believe the situation would become any easier now that the Young Turks were in power. When they espoused the creation of a national Ottoman identity, he knew they did not mean that Palestine should be divided up between the Muslims, Jews, and Christians, with each group in charge of its own autonomous slice. Instead, they intended that everyone should consider himself an Ottoman according to whatever definition the Young Turks would set. The Muslims who believed that they would now be allowed to speak Arabic in court instead of Turkish were wrong, Antebi was certain, as were the Jews who were confident that the Young Turks would tolerate any move toward Jewish autonomy in Palestine.

"The situation cannot leave us indifferent," Antebi wrote, "with these two equally threatening fires burning, one of our Ottoman authorities, and one of our young . . . fellow Jews."

In the recent vote, whose results were being celebrated that day, the Jews had not succeeded in electing even a single delegate. Ruhi Khalidi, one of three elected to represent Jerusalem, had made it clear that he planned to actively oppose not only Jewish immigration—which virtually every Arab candidate to Parliament had made a key part of his platform—but also Jewish land purchases. The Arabs' shift in emphasis toward land accumulation worried Antebi, not only because of his conviction that the steady amassing of land and the establishment of Jewish settlements was key to securing the future of the Jewish presence in Palestine, but because serving as a broker on these deals was also the only way he managed to stay financially afloat.

During the election campaign, one of the Jewish candidates had stressed the necessity of having Jewish interests represented in the new Parliament. But Antebi worried that if the Zionists continued to promote the idea of a national Jewish movement striving for political autonomy, especially in so public a forum, the situation could only grow more dangerous in Palestine. "Palestine has at most but 80,000 Jews compared to 400,000–500,000 Muslims and Christians," he told one friend about his misgivings. "Our salvation is in maintaining a good relationship with all of our fellow citizens."

But it was getting harder to sustain such relationships. After the elections, Antebi had even admitted to a friend, "If I was a Muslim Turk deputy, I would take the first opportunity to coordinate and increase restrictive measures against Jewish activity in Palestine." His assessment of the current state of affairs was the real reason he fought his way through the crowds in order to ensure that he had a front-row seat for the speeches. He wanted to hear what the newly elected Parliament member, Ruhi Khalidi, had to say.

3

Ruhi Khalidi looked out at the sea of faces, waiting for his turn to speak. He shifted nervously, the notes for his speech in the breast pocket of his shirt. He knew that he was not judged to be a brilliant orator, and suspected it was partly because he was always being compared to his famous uncle, Yusuf Khalidi, who was known for his fiery delivery. While Yusuf was quick on his feet, always ready with a joke or parable to illustrate whatever point he wanted to make, Ruhi often sank under the weight of his words.

The truth was, he considered himself primarily a writer rather than a public speaker. He loved devoting his attention to the smallest detail and could easily spend hours tracing back references in Victor Hugo's books to various sources in Arabic literature, or untangling the origins of a single word. That kind of meticulous research required an obsession with even the most seemingly insignificant point, but what was an asset in his academic career didn't always translate well into public life.

The governor of Jerusalem was still speaking, so Khalidi had a few more minutes to review his notes. He kept his face a tight mask, for even in these new, more liberal times, it remained risky to let anyone know what you were thinking, especially about a highly ranked government employee with connections back in Constantinople. Still, Khalidi fought to conceal his intense dislike of the man now standing before him and trying so determinedly to engage the crowd.

There was virtually nothing that he liked about the governor, including his choice of dress—he was all in black, as if it were a day of mourning. The governor, like all previous governors in Jerusalem, was a foreigner in town, with no connections or true ties to the city. He did not speak Arabic well and therefore insisted that everyone speak Turkish or be accompanied by a translator when transacting official business. Khalidi had found himself asking for favors from someone who could not trace his roots in Jerusalem back a hundred days, let alone a hundred years.

Khalidi had already played a role in getting the governor's predecessor, Ali Ekrem, fired. After the Young Turks had come to power in late July, official celebrations had been held throughout the empire; only in Jerusalem had there been no recognition of the new leadership. Local groups that wanted to hold their own festivities were informed by the governor's office that they did not have permission to do so, and were warned that any gathering not officially sanctioned by the governor's office would be considered illegal, its organizers subject to arrest.

For weeks the governor evaded all discussion of the subject. Perhaps he was merely being prudent, waiting to be certain that the Young Turks could actually retain their position before he committed to something as public as a celebration. In the end, Khalidi had been among those who joined in forcing his hand by signing his name to a letter addressed to the head of the Young Turks in Constantinople, asking why Jerusalem had not been allowed to celebrate, and complaining about the inexplicable tardiness of the governor in the matter. In fact, Khalidi had longtime ties to the Young Turks, and among his papers was one of the first copies of their political manifesto.

The letter had had immediate repercussions, as the governor had received a telegram urging him to sponsor the celebration Jerusalem so clearly demanded. He had readily complied, and later in a letter reporting on the event, he disputed the version circulating in Jerusalem that he had been slow to celebrate. He said that his enemies in the city had spread rumors to this effect in order to damage his reputation.

But by then, the damage had already been done; after that incident, the governor's days in Jerusalem were numbered. He had been in office for two years, not a long term, but long enough that no one would question his imminent departure. A new governor, Khalidi understood, represented a new opportunity to make his case that the Zionists' land acquisition had gone too far. In the past, Khalidi had focused his attention mainly on stopping Jewish immigration. He had signed petitions and helped lobby the governor's and sultan's offices to enact more restrictions. But even when the laws were tightened, immigrants continued to flood into Palestine, and most of them headed directly for Jerusalem. It was simply too difficult to control the influx in any meaningful way.

In the past few years, however, Khalidi's thinking on the matter had started to evolve. Even though he was now living in Constantinople, he had closely followed the changes on the ground in Jerusalem. He knew that a German Jew by the name of Arthur Ruppin had recently been dispatched to Jaffa by the Zionist Congress to set up a formal office in the country to more closely direct the purchasing of land and the establishment of Jewish settlements. On one of his visits back home, Khalidi had taken a horse and ridden out to take stock of the small Jewish towns being built outside Jerusalem. He had visited a number of settlements, even stopping in one of them, Rishon LeZion, to share a glass of wine from grapes grown in the village's famed vineyard with one of the Jewish leaders. The wine had been excellent, he noted in a report he was writing about the settlements, better than that from some of the finest vineyards in Burgundy, where he had been stationed as an Ottoman consul.

Khalidi had quickly realized that the Zionists had been buying contiguous plots of land. As soon as he left one settlement he did not have long to ride before a security guard standing outside the next one held up his hand, a weapon slung over his shoulder, to ask who he was and where he was going. That the Jews were not settling in isolated communities was a troubling development, as far as Khalidi was concerned. Concentrating their numbers by consolidating blocks of land enabled them to more effectively utilize their labor by collectively tilling the soil and planting new crops. This structure also provided a larger pool of men from which to draw for volunteer guards, who patrolled the communities on horseback at night and protected the settlers during the day while they worked in the fields, and it allowed them to establish a community hospital and run a system of Jewish schools that used Hebrew, not Turkish or Arabic, as the main language of instruction.

But unlike many of the officials to whom he took his complaints, Khalidi discerned a larger vision at work in these efforts, and this more than anything else was what disturbed him. When he met with the governor, he was told that a request had been made to the director of Mikveh Israel, the Jewish agricultural school where so many of the settlers first trained before joining other settlements, to open its doors to Muslims and Christians. The head of the school was still considering the matter, the governor assured Khalidi, but he was certain to comply.

Khalidi had little doubt that this type of strategy was doomed to failure. Everyone knew that the governor's request had been made at the behest of the Nashashibi family, one of the most powerful in Jerusalem, whose son was interested in studying agriculture at Mikveh Israel. The school, as a way of currying favor with the governor, would most likely end up admitting the boy, but what would that change? In the past few months, Khalidi had read and studied the writings of some of the key Zionist leaders. He had speeches delivered at the Zionist Congress translated into Turkish so he could more easily share them with other delegates in Parliament. He bought a copy of a book by Menachem Ussishkin, a key Zionist leader, in which Ussishkin called the Arabs "a cancer" on Palestine and urged the Jews to separate as much as possible from Arab society. He was in the process of getting it translated into Arabic as well as Turkish, and planned to circulate it widely.

These works confirmed what Khalidi had long suspected: namely, that the Zionists had a broader plan to first create a miniature state within the state, and then ultimately, when the Jews had accumulated enough land, power, and arms, to take over Palestine. It would happen without anyone's realizing what was taking place. "The aim of the Zionists," Khalidi warned, "is the creation of an Israeli kingdom whose capital will be Jerusalem."

Khalidi knew that the Zionist leaders had vociferously denied these allegations. Theodor Herzl's pursuit of a charter that would grant the Jews autonomy within Palestine had failed, the current Zionist leaders would remind the few Ottoman officials who bothered to question them about the flurry of activity in the country. At the most recent Zionist Congress, the idea of continuing to pursue a charter had been shelved, they noted. Khalidi saw this as only a temporary strategic retreat, undertaken mainly because the ascension of the Young Turks had caught the Zionist movement off guard.

All around him now, the noise of the crowd grew louder. The people burst into raucous cheers and applause for every speech, even the governor's, which was given in Turkish. And then it was Khalidi's turn. He was being drawn forward, announced to wild cheering as Jerusalem's next representative in Parliament. He stepped into the welcoming tumult and began to speak quickly. Whenever he used a certain phrase—"the rule of tyranny will end," or "we will get rid of the imperial burden"—the crowd burst out in louder and louder cheering and cries. Prior to the Young Turk revolution, these kinds of words would have been considered seditious. Even now, in the new atmosphere of freedom and the reopening of Parliament, Khalidi took a risk. But given his close connection with the Young Turks, Khalidi probably felt he could push the boundaries of his speech. The crowd clearly seemed behind him that day. Some young boys had brought drums and whistles, and the drumbeats seemed to punctuate his remarks.

When Khalidi had started his campaign for the elections, he had noted all the changes to the city. He had counted fourteen new hospitals, eleven clinics, thirty-one primary schools, five professional schools, and three asylums for the elderly and terminally ill, all established in the last few years alone. There were also many new convents, synagogues, seminaries, and religious foundations. Oil street lamps had finally appeared, and in some of the richer quarters of the city these had already been upgraded to gas lamps. In a gathering at the governor's house, Khalidi had heard rumors that the governor was negotiating with a European company to switch the city over to electricity.

The political climate of Jerusalem had changed, too. New Arabic newspapers had sprung up in the first few weeks after the Young Turk revolution and were now avidly read in Jerusalem's coffee shops and meeting places. Leaflets had begun circulating around the city that called on Arabs to stop selling their land to the Jews.

Khalidi tried to raise his voice above the din. "Even if they give an order and tell us, 'Get out, gentlemen, from this Parliament,'" he called to the crowd, "we will answer with one voice and a rushing heart!"

He offered his rallying cry again. "We will answer with one voice and a rushing heart," he told them. And then he went on, his voice rising and getting stronger, his arms lifting into the air. "We will tell them," he shouted to wild cheering that seemed to expand to fill all of Jerusalem, "we will tell them we entered this Parliament by the will of the nation and we will not leave it except through the power of arms."

4

Ruhi Khalidi had always been open to discussions with Jewish groups, including ones that he knew represented the Zionist movement. He had traveled a few years earlier to London to dine with Moses Montefiore, one of the most famous Jewish philanthropists of his day. Montefiore's riches had funded some of the most important Jewish institutions in Jerusalem, including hospitals and schools. As a young man, he had played a key role in getting Albert Antebi's grandfather released from the Damascus jail where he was falsely imprisoned. At their lunch, Khalidi had said little, although he did at one point suggest that Montefiore invest more money in institutions that would support Jerusalem's wider community, not just the Jews.

Shortly after his arrival in Constantinople in 1908, Khalidi agreed to meet with Victor Jacobson, who represented the Zionist office in the city. Khalidi was polite but made it clear to Jacobson that he did not support Zionist aims in Palestine. The following year, he gave an interview to Eliezer Ben Yehuda, the man most responsible for the revival of spoken Hebrew in Palestine, which ran in Ben Yehuda's Hebrew newspaper in Jerusalem. In their conversation, he expanded on the idea he had first raised with Montefiore. He complained to Ben Yehuda that the Jews had made little effort to "draw closer" to the Arabs. By focusing on the revival of Hebrew rather than learning Arabic language and culture, and by not hiring

Arabs to work on the land they bought and the settlements they established, they were intentionally separating themselves from the mainstream of Palestine, and only reinforcing local fears that the Jews had come to dispossess the Arabs.

In that interview, Ruhi Khalidi stated a belief that he continued to repeat for years afterward: namely, that the Jews actually possessed no more rights than anyone else to the land of Palestine, and in fact, fewer rights than the Arabs had. "We did not conquer this land from you," Khalidi told the reporter. "We conquered it from the Byzantines who ruled it then. We do not owe anything to the Jews. The Jews were not here when we conquered the country."

In May 1911 Khalidi saw an opportunity to take his concerns to the wider public. A debate was then under way in Parliament regarding the proposed budget for the Ministry of the Interior, and Khalidi put his name down on the list of representatives wanting to speak that day. The Arab deputies had agreed earlier that something needed to be said about the situation in Jerusalem and in the rest of Palestine. Khalidi had helped them prepare, and they had seen to it that the French translation of a book by Jacobus Kann, an executive member of the Zionist Congress, was distributed to other members of Parliament. In that book, Kann had called for the formation of a Jewish army. "If we want peace, we shall have to prepare for war," he had written.

When it came time for Khalidi's turn to speak, he stood before the assembly and asserted that he was not an anti-Semite, but rather an anti-Zionist. Then he and the two other deputies from Jerusalem proceeded to lay out their case. They described how Kann's ideas were being adopted in Palestine, as Jews were now training in militias. They presented the translation Khalidi had made of "Hatikvah," the Jewish national anthem that was now routinely sung at Jewish schools and before any meeting of Jewish groups. Khalidi's fellow Jerusalem delegate Said Husseini passed around to the assembly what he called "Jewish stamps," which featured portraits of Herzl and other Zionist movement leaders. All these actions, they argued, indicated that the Jews had already taken major steps toward setting up the rudiments of their own state. When would the Parliament act to stop them?

In opposition, Vartkes Hovhannes Serengülyan, the Armenian deputy from the town of Erzerum, stood and protested that the Jerusalem delegates were trying to create a "Jewish question" in the empire where none existed. "Formerly, hatred of the Armenians was created," Vartkes accused the men. "Now you want to inculcate hatred of the Jews into the people." Hafiz Ibrahim, the deputy from Albania, insisted there was nothing to fear from so-called Jewish militias. The idea that the Jews in Palestine could militarily take over the country now or in the future was inconceivable, he declared.

In the end, the most the assembled delegates agreed to do was to pass a resolution calling for the strict application of its already existing regulations preventing land sales to foreigners. It had not been the victory that Khalidi had wanted but he urged his colleagues to regard what had happened that day as a kind of victory. The Parliament had agreed with their key point—that the laws against land sales to foreigners in Palestine should be rigorously enforced.

Not surprisingly, Khalidi's parliamentary speech produced panic in the Jewish community in Jerusalem. Rumors spread that the Arabs were plotting a massacre. Albert Antebi had petitioned at the governor's office so many times that the governor finally agreed to his request to adopt security measures to protect the Jews. He brought a large force of police from Jaffa, who patrolled the Jewish neighborhoods until the storm of fear caused by the Parliament debate started to abate.

Antebi knew that these latest developments left the governor with no choice but to take action to try to prevent the sale of land to non-Ottoman Jews, but he nevertheless wanted to guarantee that Jews who were Ottoman citizens still retained the right to purchase property. He accordingly came up with a solution: he agreed to make a list of Ottoman Jews whom he trusted, names which he would personally vet. The list would be submitted to the governor for approval, and these men then would be allowed to purchase large tracts of land in Jerusalem and other areas of Palestine.

The Arab delegates objected to the plan; the men Antebi had selected were all sympathetic to the Zionist cause. They would allow the Zionists to establish cities and to continue with their plans to create an autonomous Jewish part of Palestine. This would not stop the threat of dispossession of the Arabs. Their complaints in Parliament made no difference, however, which to Khalidi only highlighted the powerlessness of the Arab delegates. Palestine's fate was being decided by everyone but the majority of people who lived there. Khalidi was not aware what Max Nordau, whose face was on one of the Zionist stamps he and the others had distributed the day of the debate in Parliament, had said to Victor Jacobson, when Jacobson told him he was meeting with Khalidi in Constantinople in an effort to find some common ground. Nordau had told Jacobson to go ahead, and to meet with Khalidi, if that was what he wanted to do. But he added, "The keys to the house which we Zionists want to make our national home are in the hands of the Turkish government"—not someone like Ruhi Khalidi.

5

Albert Antebi had always considered himself an optimistic man, someone who could talk himself out of trouble or come up with a solution to a problem that left both sides in a dispute satisfied. But lately, even he could not shake the feeling that something terrible was about to happen. After Ruhi Khalidi's fiery speech in the Parliament, Antebi had received telegrams, letters, and even some late-night visits from the concerned Jews of Jerusalem.

In the end, Antebi felt he had once again succeeded in keeping the peace, as the anticipated clashes in the wake of the speech did not touch Jerusalem. But all throughout Palestine, particularly in areas where a Jewish settlement had been built next to an Arab village, tensions ran high, and there were increasingly frequent reports of violence. The promise of unity of the 1908 revolution had failed. Jerusalem was becoming Babel, a place whose inhabitants spoke different languages, talked at one another but did not understand a word of what the other was saying. Eventually, the tower of Babel had been destroyed, and its people scattered to separate corners of the earth and a destiny of incomprehension. Was that ultimately going to be Jerusalem's fate as well?

By the start of 1912, Antebi's outlook on the continuance of good relations between the Jews and their neighbors in Palestine was bleak. He had always promoted closer cooperation with the Muslims but was now repeatedly rebuffed by his Jewish friends. They saw a future in a revival of Jewish national life, rather than in fighting for the full rights that the new Ottoman constitution guaranteed them.

When he had proposed to some of his wealthy Jewish friends who wanted to start a newspaper that it should be published in Arabic and French, in order to draw both Muslim and Jewish readers, they had turned him down. They had suggested a Hebrew and French paper instead, in order to help revive Jewish culture in Palestine. He had urged the leaders of the Zionist-run Anglo-Palestine Bank not only to buy more land for Jews but to create a bridge to better relations with the Arabs. When the bank's officers had responded to this idea and started making more loans to Arabs in Jerusalem, they had been taken to task by Jewish groups who opposed the concept.

Antebi had very little confidence in the Zionists, who despite the rising tensions in the city continued to demand that Jews replace the Arab workers who had once performed many tasks on Jewish settlements. Antebi had argued with his Zionist friends over the practicality of the idea. For one thing, Jewish workers demanded higher wages than Arabs. Given that the settlements were already financially overextended, hiring more expensive workers when an ample supply of cheaper labor was available made no economic sense. But it also made no political sense, as Antebi stressed. It was far more practical to show the Muslims that they had a stake in the success of the Jewish farms. Antebi was certain that many of the current confrontations between the two groups arose from this move to replace Arab workers, who now saw their livelihoods threatened.

But the Zionists kept pushing their own agenda during that fall of 1912. An association called Talpiot was founded, to try to raise funds to build a new neighborhood for Jews near the Jerusalem railroad station, where trains arrived every day from Jaffa. Instead of the mixed communities that once had characterized neighborhoods in the Old City, Arabs and Jews now started living more frequently in their own segregated neighborhoods. An American rabbi with ties to the Zionists, Judah Magnes, had been promoting and raising funds to build a Jewish academic institute in Jerusalem, which he and his followers hoped would serve as a core for their ultimate goal, a full-fledged Jewish university, where courses would be taught in Hebrew. "The rebuilding of Jerusalem has begun," A. M. Luncz, the publisher of the annual calendar that chronicled events in the city, told Antebi.

In the Arabic press, which Antebi read every week to try to gauge the opinion of the Arab community, news of such grandiose plans inspired not only fear and bitterness, but a drive toward resistance and confrontation on the part of Muslim groups. "If this state of affairs continues," Arif al-Arif, publisher of one of the key Arabic-language papers, wrote, "then the Zionists will gain mastery over our country, village by village, town by town." "Tomorrow," he warned his faithful readers, "the whole of Jerusalem will be sold."

As 1912 drew to a close, Antebi began questioning his own faith in the strategy of promoting Jewish economic power and the campaign to gain their full rights as loyal Ottomans. When the Zionist movement had first started in Jerusalem, he had dismissed it, believing their noisy nationalism was dangerous. And yet increasingly he understood the appeal Zionism seemed to have for so many people in Jerusalem and beyond.

By the start of 1913 the promise of the Young Turk revolution was dimming. Expectations had fallen short, and the goal of Jews being considered Ottoman citizens had not been realized. Antebi had tried in the previous years to get the governor to lift some of the most restrictive regulations against Jews, such as that prohibiting them from climbing higher than the seventh step when visiting Abraham's cave in Hebron. The governor had claimed his hands were tied, that any changes in such a long-standing and sensitive tradition might provoke a riot among the Muslims living there. Antebi had also lobbied to have the Ottoman military band play in the city square during the festive holiday of Purim, just as it did during Christian and Muslim holidays. "We will not be considered less than the Christians," he had declared. The governor had promised that he would make every effort to get that change made, and had succeeded. The band performed on the Jewish holidays, playing the Ottoman anthem, as well as a number of Jewish religious tunes. There were rumors that they even knew how to play "Hatikvah." But these were very minor victories and fell far short of the expectations set when the Young Turks had come to power.

Given the state of affairs, Antebi believed the Zionist appeal to the wider public would only continue to rise. The Zionists offered a kind of solace for the damaged national pride of the Jews, combined with a muscular vision of how things ought to be instead. It was an unsettling combination. One evening Antebi wrote a letter to an old friend in which he poured out his rising fears. "Would someone like to write an epilogue about my hopes for the future?" he concluded.

Everywhere he looked, Antebi realized that the leaders of the various Jewish and Arab groups pressed ahead with their own agendas, while no one tried to stop the inexorable march toward conflict. They were all "sleeping on volcanoes, of which minorities guard the craters," he wrote in one warning. Would anyone listen to him now? If not, he feared the consequences for Jerusalem's future. "If one does not have open eyes, a volcano could explode," he concluded, "without even a warning sound."

PART THREE

Jerusalem 1913

The danger is clear
Can no one resist it?
Is there not an eye left
To shed a tear for our country?

—SHEIKH SULAYMAN AL-TAJI

Arthur Ruppin had served as head of the Palestine Office since it first opened its doors on Bustrus Street in Jaffa in 1908, shortly after the Young Turks had seized power and taken over the Ottoman government. But it was only in January 1913 that he and his subordinates authored a memo that came to define and help shape the strategic thinking of the Zionists for years to come.

At first glance, Ruppin seemed an unlikely candidate for the position. A successful, self-made German lawyer, he was never seen without a suit and tie. He had used his talent for the law as a way out of dire poverty and now lived a comfortable existence. After a visit to Palestine, however, he decided to move there, for no matter how successful he became in Germany, he always felt like an outsider. In Palestine, he could help create something new and shape it at least in part in his own image.

After arriving in Jaffa he struggled to accommodate to his new life. He had given up smoking through sheer willpower, but then took it up again after a few months in his new home because the smoke kept the mosquitoes away when he visited the newly established farms to check on the Jewish settlers' progress. When he realized that it would be impossible for him to travel to the far-flung Jewish settlements except by horse, he taught himself how to ride. He knew his struggles to mount the horse made him look slightly ridiculous, and at the end of an arduous day of travel he felt stiff with pain. But the long trips on horseback throughout the country helped him learn the terrain.

Ruppin rented a small apartment on Bustrus Street, in the heart of the commercial district of Jaffa. He had briefly considered Jerusalem as the site for the new office, but quickly rejected it. As a practical matter, that city still seemed mired in the tensions between the older, more religious community of Jews who had been settled there for generations and the more recent arrivals, the Zionists, who were struggling to articulate and implement a national identity. Ruppin was worried that those tensions would be a distraction from his mission.

Jaffa was closer than Jerusalem, not just physically but also temperamentally, to the settlements that had already been set up in the northern section of the country. It was also where some of the wealthiest Arab landowners came to enjoy the nightlife and, more important, from Ruppin's perspective, to make deals. When Ruppin needed to check out the site of some land he wanted to buy or drop in on one of the settlements that the office was supporting, or quietly meet a prospective landowner who he heard might be willing to sell some of his properties to Jews in Palestine, it was easier to get a train, hire a horse, or secure a berth on a small ship headed to Beirut from Jaffa than from virtually any other city in Palestine. Jaffa also offered more possibilities for an enterprise like the Palestine Office.

Bustrus Street itself was located in a lively section of the city, within walking distance of the port where the new Jewish immigrants who continued to make their way to Palestine first landed, and everywhere one looked there seemed to be a coffee shop where groups of young people met to talk politics or carry on animated literary discussions. Some of the most famous Jewish writers of the time, men like Chaim Brenner and S. Y. Agnon, who during this period were starting to publish stories about the new pioneers in Palestine in a revitalized Hebrew, had regular tables at the Bustrus Café. The new Hebrew daily newspapers, such as *HaPoel* and *Ha-Herut*, were delivered to the cafés and eagerly passed from hand to hand, then left behind on the tables at the end of the day, as if worn out from so many readings.

Here Ruppin felt at home among the other new immigrants streaming into Palestine. Jaffa was built on the edge of the sea, not on rocks, as Jerusalem was, and the smell of saltwater from the harbor mixed with the sticky sweet odor of oranges from the heavily laden fruit trees that ringed the city and were the engine of its prosperity. Sometimes Jaffa seemed like a large garden, with virtually every home boasting lush fruit trees and flowers. Ruppin liked to walk to the beach and stare out at the sea, his mind free to wander over the possibilities of life in Palestine.

For many of the new immigrants, Arthur Ruppin's headquarters was the first stop after disembarking. There they might cadge a loan, or get a ride to a job on a new settlement, or simply hear some of the gossip about those they knew from home who had arrived in Palestine before them. Ruppin had made a point almost from the very beginning of staffing the Palestine Office mainly with Jews who were Ottoman citizens and native Arabic speakers, a language he found difficult to master. (It took him years even to learn how to speak passable Hebrew, despite his prominent role in helping to lay the groundwork for the foundation of the Jewish state.) He firmly believed that, when given the choice, it was almost always better to send a native Arabic speaker to negotiate on behalf of the Palestine Office. So many of the tensions between Jews and Arabs, Ruppin was convinced, grew out of simple miscommunication, a subtle and perhaps even unintended insult that one side or the other made because they were unfamiliar with the other's language, customs, or religion. He never worried about this issue with native Arabic speakers, who had lived in parts of the Ottoman Empire often for generations. They knew how to get along with their neighbors; they were usually able to close a deal, or, if not, to leave matters in a cordial way to be discussed another day.

He felt so strongly on this subject that, despite his conviction that the Zionists needed to settle as much land as possible as quickly as they could, he turned down a request by a group of Russians who asked to be granted a plot of land near the Jordan River for a settlement because, he explained, the Arabs who lived there had not had much interaction or experience with Jews, and it was preferable that a group of Arabic-speaking Jews settle there first and establish good relations. "Unpleasant incidents between Arabs and Jews in Palestine keep occurring simply because the Jew understands neither the language nor the customs of the Arab and the Arab views with animosity what has in reality to be ascribed to the Jew's ignorance," Ruppin wrote to the group's leader in explanation. Once more Jews had settled there and the Arabs grew accustomed to their new neighbors, the Russians would be free to go there too, he promised.

It was clear that Ruppin regarded 1913 as a turning point—the year that a strategic design would emerge for how the Jews would get along with the Arabs. He understood instinctively that it was the Arabs and not the Turks who were the key obstacle to Jewish plans, since they were the main competitors for control of the land of Palestine, and what was decided in 1913 would come to shape the future of Arab-Jewish relations in Palestine for decades to come. He quickly found himself at the very center of the emerging confrontation. His views were not in the mainstream at first, but he articulated them so crisply, and saw the issues so sharply, that in the end his sense of imminent crisis and his perception that the conflict with the Arabs could no longer be ignored set the larger agenda.

It was Ruppin's idea to focus Jewish land-buying in areas that were close together, rather than scattered far apart, recognizing not only that they might someday form the border of a Jewish homeland but that, in the event of military conflict, they would be easier for a Jewish army to defend. In an effort to avert a workers' strike at one of the settlements, Ruppin came up with the compromise that would drive the future development of Israel: the creation of the kvutzah, or collective settlement, now known as a kibbutz. This kind of thinking did not go unnoticed in the Zionist movement. "Suddenly people are for or against me," wrote Ruppin in his diary in 1913, summing up the change, "seeing me as a personification of the good or the bad principle of our activities in Palestine."

What that principle was, exactly, had found no real agreement yet, although in 1913 the shape of it began to coalesce, in an exchange of letters and reports between the various Zionist movement officials scattered through Europe, Palestine, and Constantinople, largely because of the efforts of Ruppin and the small circle of men he gathered around him. Victor Jacobson, who was Ruppin's counterpart at the Zionist office in Constantinople, took a somewhat different approach. In his reports to the Zionist Congress's head, David Wolffsohn, he explained that whether he spoke to other Jews in Constantinople or government officials, his tactic was the same: "The important thing is the emphasis that we have no separatist aims, no plans for political action in the land." Jacobson, the ideal diplomat, believed in working behind the scenes and never tipping one's hand or being too candid. He was certain that this applied as much to his own natural constituents, Jews around the world, as to the Ottoman government, a sentiment with which Ruppin agreed.

When Wolffsohn and some of the other Zionist leaders proposed holding the 1913 Zionist Congress in Constantinople, Jacobson was among the most vociferous in protesting such a move. The sultan, as well as all his officials, would be totally opposed to so visible an influx into the Ottoman capital of Zionists discussing the establishment of a Jewish homeland in Palestine. Only bad could come out of such a move, Jacobson argued. Wolffsohn capitulated, and they chose instead Vienna, Herzl's hometown, as the site for the conference, slated for that September. When a book written by a leading Zionist leader, Jacobus Kann, was published, calling for the establishment of a Jewish army in order to achieve Zionism's aims, it was quickly translated into French at the behest of Ruhi Khalidi and other Palestinian nationalists in order to alert the wider public to a more militant side of Zionism. Jacobson lamented the situation in another letter. "It is clear that our aims will be seen as incompatible with the integrity of the Ottoman Empire."

This attitude was firmly in keeping with the very philosophy that defined Jacobson's existence: if someone is not naturally inclined to be on your side, you must do everything in your power to guarantee that he does not actively work against you. Jacobson had, for example, recently asked the chief rabbi in Constantinople to publicly declare that the Zionists held no separatist aspirations—a request the rabbi declined.

Ruppin always took careful note of Jacobson's efforts and at times agreed with his tactic of dissembling when necessary. But the recent exchange between Jacobson and the chief rabbi had galvanized Ruppin. With his legalistic mind, he considered all the implications of the chief rabbi's refusal to take a public stand on the Zionist movement, and his conclusion was unequivocal. The chief rabbi was not a Zionist, but it was assumed by Ruppin and the others that he would be supportive of a movement for Jewish cultural renewal. The fact was that the rabbi had already decided that Zionism was a potentially revolutionary movement, despite whatever assurances to the contrary that well-spoken, cultivated Zionist officials like Jacobson had given him. Trying now to convince him otherwise was clearly a waste of time.

Ruppin faithfully read the articles that the office regularly translated from the Arabic press, and he tried to keep track of what was happening in the wider empire with an eye to how it might affect the Zionist movement's goals in Palestine. The conclusion he reached—independently at first but then buttressed by discussions both at work and afterward at his regular table at the Bustrus

Café—was that the Zionist stronghold in Palestine was in grave danger. This belief was one of the key factors that distinguished Ruppin from virtually everyone else in the Palestine Office. Most of its staff had always lived among the Arabs, felt comfortable in the Muslim culture of the Ottoman Empire, and did not see any reason why that had to change, even with the advent of Zionism. When they wrote articles about Zionism for the Arabic press, they were heartfelt in arguing that there was no reason for the Arabs to fear the Zionists, that Zionism was more of a cultural renaissance than a nationalist movement, that it was possible to be both a Zionist and a loyal Ottoman, and that the relations between Muslims and Jews did not have to change. Ruppin, however, saw the matter differently, and suspected that if the Arabs shared his concern—and the evidence he saw from newspaper articles and his own travels around the country indicated that they did—then the Zionists would have to move much more quickly than before in order to consolidate their gains before conflict broke out.

Moreover, in January 1913, the Ottoman Empire had begun to face serious political conflict—both at home and abroad. The previous year, Serbia, Bulgaria, and Greece had formed a Balkan League, created explicitly with the hope of reclaiming from the Ottomans some of the European territories captured in past wars. In October 1912, after months of agitation opposing Ottoman rule in his land, King Nicholas of Montenegro declared war against the sultan, and a week later the three other Balkan states joined in. They demanded that all the European provinces then controlled by the Ottomans be granted ethnic autonomy, which essentially was a call for the end of the empire. The Ottoman army mobilized, but the situation deteriorated. Facing heavy losses, the Ottoman empire acceded to an armistice and peace talks began.

The Young Turks were also facing opposition at home. The Entente Liberale party formed, and the majority of the Arab deputies elected to the Ottoman Parliament in the 1908 elections now joined. (Ruhi Khalidi was not among them; he still supported the Young Turks.) The main grievances of the opposition focused on the lack of autonomy for ethnic groups, particularly Arabs, who wanted more control over their daily lives in cities where they formed the majority of the population. In July 1912, elections were held and the Entente Liberale party came to power.

Then in January 1913, just a few weeks before Ruppin's office drafted its memo about Zionist strategy in Palestine, the Young Turks staged another coup and returned to power. In a raid on the Sublime Porte, where the sultan's palace stood and the government regularly held its cabinet sessions, rebels led by one of the Young Turks, Ismail Enver, burst into the cabinet meeting, and shot and killed the minister of war on the spot. Reshid Bey, the former governor of Jerusalem and one of Albert Antebi's closest friends, was one of the witnesses to the brutal killing. He, along with the rest of the cabinet members, was told to resign immediately or pay with his life. The entire group acceded to the demand.

The country was now led by a powerful triumvirate that would remain in power until after the Ottoman Empire's defeat in World War I: Ismail Enver, Mehmed Talat, and Ahmed Djemal. One of the new government's first acts was to resume the fighting against the Balkan League in the hope of winning back some of the lost territory. In March 1913, however, the Ottoman troops who had held out in Adrianople, one of the last remaining Ottoman strongholds, were finally forced to surrender to the Bulgarian-Serbian army. While Ismail Enver eventually won back Adrianople, becoming a war hero in the process, by the time the May 1913 Treaty of London finally ended the conflict, the Ottoman Empire had lost all its remaining European possessions, other than a small area around Constantinople. Twenty percent of the empire's population was suddenly depatriated.

Even before the peace treaty was signed, though, Ruppin feared that the latest events could only harm the Zionist efforts in Palestine. For one thing, having lost its European provinces, the Ottoman Empire would now be overwhelmingly Muslim. In Ruppin's view, the government would either have to crack down completely on any sign of nationalism, for fear that it would threaten the stability of the now truncated empire, or it would have to be much more receptive to Arab insistence on greater power, as a way of heading off any more serious encroachments by what was now their most important constituency. The government, Ruppin surmised, would consequently be even more reluctant to agree to Jewish demands for more immigration to Palestine and a loosening of the restrictions on Jews buying large swaths of land there. Whatever the result of the war, one Palestine Office memo analyzing the situation concluded, "the Arabs will emerge from this . . . crisis strengthened."

The January 1913 memo that the Palestine Office had prepared assessed the previous two years of work in Palestine and judged them successes. A "considerable area," the report stated, had been obtained in that short period by the Zionists, almost 50,000 dunams, throughout the country. Jewish property ownership in key cities, such as Jerusalem, had also increased. These purchases were necessary, the report went on, "to strengthen ourselves for the expected less favorable time."

Even with these substantial gains, however, the Jews still did not own enough property to sustain a Jewish homeland in Palestine. In order to do so, they needed to continue to acquire parcels from Arab landowners. But "if the Arab national consciousness is strengthened," the report concluded, "then we will encounter resistance that can perhaps no longer be resolved with money. . . . If the Arabs gather themselves up to consider it a national disgrace and betrayal to sell their land to Jews, then the situation will become a pretty difficult one for us."

Palestine Office officials had argued in their report for a full-blown effort to accumulate as much property as possible, and as quickly as possible, and then bring in as many new immigrants as they could, before it was too late. "It is extraordinarily lamentable that this moment is understood so little by our followers. What we neglect to achieve now, we will perhaps never be able to obtain."

Beginning in 1913, Ruppin urged an abandonment of Victor Jacobson's careful smokescreen that Zionism had no separatist aims when speaking with Jews around the world. Jewish communities should be told clearly what was at stake, and why their assistance was needed. Without more money to buy land, and without more Jews willing to move to Palestine to work it, Zionism was doomed to fail. There would be no Jewish homeland unless the Jews openly and aggressively tried to create one.

Within Palestine, he argued for at least trying to explain some of the Zionists' positions. For instance, on his support for employing primarily Jewish workers in the settlements, he suggested that it be made clear that "only if we create 'a work of our own hands' in Palestine and not by the exploitation of alien labour will we earn for ourselves a moral right to the land which we have legally acquired." "This makes it clear that the employment of Jewish workers does not in any way indicate hostility to the Arabs," he added, "but is brought about by our endeavour to train ourselves to work and to fertilize our land with our own sweat."

Ruppin felt that just as the Zionist movement was growing, so was the Arab movement. The fact that the Arabs in Palestine had come to see themselves as a separate entity from the Ottomans with a stake in the country's future and a desire to shape it only posed a threat to Zionist goals there. "As yet the Arabs are not organized and not strong enough to be feared by us as a present danger," the Palestine Office report concluded. But that would quickly change, Ruppin and his colleagues felt. "We must be clear that we are living through a critical moment," said the report, and behind this statement one could hear Ruppin's ideas as he held forth in the Bustrus Café. "We will have to reckon with an enemy that will need to be taken very seriously in the near future."

2

In 1913, Ruhi Khalidi made a series of trips throughout Palestine, which became the basis for his latest book, which he titled *Zionism or the Zionist Question*. He hoped to publish it, one more volume in the expanding literature wrestling with the implications of the growing conflict with the Zionists that was emerging around this time, but never succeeded in that goal. The manuscript was found among the papers of one of Khalidi's brothers after he died, and has remained in the family's possession ever since.

Given his interests, it is almost certain that Khalidi read the key contemporary Arab works that addressed Zionism. The most famous was Najib Ajouri's *The Arab Awakening*, first published in French in 1905 but still circulating in Jerusalem years later, which predicted violent confrontation between the Jews and the Muslims for control of Palestine. Another major work was a collection of pieces that first ran as a series of articles in the newspaper *Al Najjar*, whose forceful rhetoric against Zionism and calls for boycotts of any Arab who sold his land to the Jews had gotten the paper banned from time to time by the Ottoman authorities, as they feared its potential to incite violence.

As a rising star in the Ottoman government—by now he was the deputy to the head of Parliament—Khalidi was acutely aware of the political repercussions involved with even writing about a nationalistic movement, especially as the Ottoman Empire found itself drawn into conflicts sparked by uprisings in various of its territories. He accordingly kept his manuscript a secret, carefully packing it away and taking it with him on his frequent travels between Constantinople and Jerusalem. By the spring of 1913, he had already filled two volumes, his handwriting and observations spreading out across the pages of foolscap that piled next to him as he wrote.

Zionism or the Zionist Question was a wide-ranging analysis that drew not only on Khalidi's reading of the Hebrew Bible, but on his firsthand encounters with settlers. It was that immediacy that distinguishes his work from the other polemics of this period. As a member of Parliament, Khalidi could not be turned away from the gates of a Jewish settlement, and he made a point of visiting as many as possible. He often gave no advance notice of his appearance, but might unexpectedly show up at the start of the day, when the workers were sitting under the trees eating their morning breakfast of eggs, tomatoes, and bread, with a sticky sweet piece of halvah saved in wax paper as a sugary treat. He was eager to see what the crops were yielding, and sometimes convinced one of the farmers to show him the new techniques they were trying to increase their harvests. The Jewish settlers were proud of their methods and interested in talking about their work, and Khalidi's observations were filled both with fear and admiration for the success he saw they were having.

As the months passed, he walked between the groves of trees in Rehovot, and saw them filled with almonds that would be picked and piled up in huge stacks, then shelled at a daylong festival that drew people from all over the area, including the Arab villages whose residents made money helping out with the shelling. He knew that when the governor of Jerusalem was escorted by Albert Antebi to Rishon LeZion, twenty horsemen, their weapons held high in salute, came out to greet him. He knew that the governor had given a speech in French praising the accomplishments of the Jewish settlers, and granting them more land on which to expand. Khalidi

noticed how each of the settlements had its own pharmacy and synagogue. When he visited the settlement of Ekron, he described it in
his book with evocative language, as if it were a kind of mirage in the
desert—a place, he wrote, filled with "beautiful houses whose red
roofs shine with the rays of the hot sun," and whose "well maintained roads . . . are lined with trees."

Often, Khalidi rode to the south of Jerusalem, down the winding
paths and purple mountains that led into the desert, where the Bedouin tribes were encamped. He knew that Arthur Ruppin's Palestine
Office was also buying land there, in an effort to expand the network
of Jewish settlements, with Jerusalem as the heart that connected
the northern and southern parts of the country. On those visits,
Khalidi collected data like a lawyer, and tried to build a case against
the Zionists and the way that they bought land. The sale of land in
Palestine had always been rife with corruption and shady dealing.
Less than a third of the country was even considered cultivatable, so
there was a great deal of competition for choice parcels. The rest
was mainly enormous stretches that sat on sand or on marshes, that
did not get enough water, or simply for one reason or another could
not be tilled effectively. Crop yields were low, and even then it was
a challenge to get everything harvested in time because men were
always subject to sudden conscription for one of the empire's many
wars—sometimes plucked off the fields as they picked crops by soldiers looking to recruit more bodies. Given all these difficulties, it
was almost impossible to maintain a regular workforce.

For the wealthy families that constituted the elite in Jerusalem,
like the Khalidis, the Nashashibis, and the Husseinis, land was the
main source of wealth. The very techniques that the Jews were now
using to acquire property had been practiced by the Arabs. These
dynasties also had a vast network of family members in high and
important government positions, and were therefore in frequent
personal contact with key officials. When prime land went on the

market, these families were among the first to know, and with the rents they collected from their properties, they were able to acquire even more. Other family members worked in the various government offices that processed the paperwork and red tape involved with any land registration applications and helped determine the fate of land that was in dispute.

The land system was also subject to fraud and abuse because smaller farmers, who were leery of contact with government officials, often failed to register their land, fearing that giving the government too much information about their holdings might result in higher taxes, or perhaps a conscription notice for one or all of their sons. If they did register it, they would understate the actual size of the parcel to avoid being taxed at the full amount. Sometimes they used a reference from one of the elite families, who promised to run interference with the government, but then found themselves the victims of trickery or the sort of behind-the-scenes deals that marked almost all of the major land sales of this period.

Khalidi's objections to the Jews' taking advantage of the very system through which his own social circle had acquired much of its wealth might seem cynical. And in reading his pages, it does seem that he turned a blind eye to practices followed by those with whom he identified or felt a sense of kinship, while at the same time decrying them when employed by the Zionists. But Khalidi, a political man, saw the world in a particular way. To him, there was something different about what the Jews were doing, and the difference, as he saw it, lay in their intentions.

The Muslim landowners, for all their power and their riches, remained part of the existing political system, even while they benefited personally from their transactions. But the Jewish land purchasers did not seek to gain power within the system. Their acquisition of land, rather, was designed to subvert it from within, since their goal was the creation of their own state. The fact that corrupt Ottoman officials colluded with them, and allowed them to continue buying huge swaths of land, either without seeing or without caring about the ultimate consequences, was the source of Khalidi's deepest frustration and his rising anger. In the pages of his book it is possible to conjure up a picture of him during this period from his handwriting—the tight script suggests a fury that is still leashed, while the pages filled with stops and starts reveal how he was compelled to steal snatches of time to write his unguarded thoughts about the corruption he saw all around him, undermining the future of the Muslims in Palestine.

He recorded how the magistrate in Gaza would claim that a given piece of land belonged to him, and when the true owner, a farmer or peasant, protested, he would be thrown in jail until he complied with the magistrate's falsehood. The magistrate, working with a collaborator in the land office, would have the land officially registered in his own name, and then turn around and immediately sell it to the Jews, who were willing to pay high prices to acquire it.

In March 1913, on a visit to a Bedouin village, one of the village leaders read a poem aloud. It described how the tribe was slowly losing its land through these methods. Khalidi carefully recorded the words of the poem in his book. "Some Bedouin sheiks oppress their subjects," the Bedouin poet sang, as the others sat solemnly around him listening. "And there is the sale of tribal land / And wine has come to us and the misguided drink it . . . / This is why there is ruination of our people / And the sale of our entire estate [milk] to the Jews."

Khalidi was not an Arab nationalist in the sense that we have come to understand this word—he was a man who still saw his destiny as being firmly tied to that of the Ottoman Empire. He recognized that the growth of Zionism was being fueled in part by rabid anti-Semitism in Europe. He saw the Jews as threatening to Palestine, but he also knew that they themselves felt threatened. He realized that Zionism derived some of its influence from tapping into the very real fear that Jews had of being persecuted in their native countries, always treated as second-class citizens no matter how hard they tried to fit in.

Khalidi wrestled in his writings with the question of whether Judaism was strictly a religion or if it could be considered a legitimate nationality. No nation longed for Zion like the Jews had, Khalidi wrote. He knew that at the end of prayers and gatherings Jews would often cry out in Hebrew, "Next year in Jerusalem!"—a sentiment that also ended each Zionist Congress. Khalidi did not regard this as an empty slogan, but as further proof that the Jews had, in his words, a "strong insistence on owning" Jerusalem.

In Jerusalem itself, tensions between the Arabs and Jews continued to rise. In March 1913, some Jewish members of the Temple of Solomon Masonic lodge broke off to found a new lodge, which they called Moriah. There, only French, not Arabic, was spoken. Jews constituted the vast majority—over 60 percent—of its membership.

A rift arose between the rival lodges and quickly grew acrimonious. Even though all of the Jewish members who had left the Temple of Solomon for the new lodge had been born in the Ottoman Empire—including two in Jerusalem itself—they explained that one reason they had departed was that the Muslims had routinely called them foreigners at meetings. The Jews accused their former fellow lodge members of being suspicious of Zionism because it was considered a Western movement, while they viewed supporting it as a way of affirming Jewish culture and pride.

In a letter written to the Masonic headquarters in Paris by a Muslim member of the Temple of Solomon seeking to prevent the rival lodge from gaining official recognition, the Moriah lodge was described as filled with Zionists, "an Israelite society having particularistic ambitions in Palestine." The letter writer went on to add that the Muslim members did not want to be seen socializing with or affiliating in any way with people considered Zionists. Each side complained that the other voted as a bloc and vetoed their suggestions.

Khalidi's concern about the nationalistic discord growing in Jerusalem began to be shared by the city's people, who now felt forced to choose sides. Even the notion of a mixed lodge was starting to seem like part of another era. The amount of common space in Jerusalem, owned and controlled by no one, operated through negotiation and the artful compromise, was rapidly shrinking. When he reflected on all he saw taking place in Jerusalem, Khalidi wrote with resignation, "A new nationalism is growing—where there was none before."

3

It began, Albert Antebi explained, as "a simple brawl over the theft of a bunch of grapes" but quickly "degenerated into a double murder." That incident just outside the Jewish settlement of Rehovot, in July 1913, came to dominate newspaper headlines and the chatter in the Jerusalem cafés where Antebi still liked to wile away many afternoons.

In its report to the Zionist Central Office in Berlin about the confrontation in Rehovot, the Palestine Office characterized the event as merely "a sad incident," not wanting to cause further alarm or raise suspicions back in Berlin that the violence was endemic. "Some Arab camel drivers from Zarnuqa, a neighboring village to Rehovot, were bringing goods to the Jewish settlement," the report recounted. On the way, they entered one of the settlements and stole some grapes. "The guard chased them away," the report described, "but was robbed of his weapon in the process." When the guard called for help, others gave chase after the camel drivers to retrieve the gun.

The sequence of events that led up to the shooting then became less clear. It appeared that a struggle broke out between the Jews and Arabs on the road between the two settlements, and other Arabs from Zarnuqa, hearing the cries, came over to help. "The scuffle became a shoot out," the report went on.

A camel and a horse belonging to the Arabs and a horse belonging to the Jews were shot—as were several people, including one Arab who later died of his wounds. The list of injuries to Jews relayed in the report indicated that the Arabs had grabbed whatever they could find and rushed over to the scene of the fight—one Jew was wounded by a blow to his head with a saber, a second with a large club smashed on the shoulder, a third was shot in the stomach. As a result of the incident at least one Jewish guard was in prison and more arrests were expected.

Then, shortly afterward, a Jewish guard in Rehovot was murdered, and another report was sent to Berlin: "The victim was a strong young man of about 23, full of zest of life and previously a pupil at the sculpture academy in Paris, who had emigrated to Palestine only half a year ago." At first the guard's murder was thought to be an act of revenge by the villagers of Zarnuqa, in retaliation for the murder of the Arab farmer. Later, though, Rehovot's leaders came to believe that the guard had been killed when he caught a thief in the act of stealing almonds. Suspects had been arrested in this case, as well, and a trial was expected shortly.

Rehovot had already spent more than 7,000 francs hiring lawyers and providing lost income to the families touched by the incident. At the Palestine Office Arthur Ruppin fielded a steady stream of telegrams and letters from distraught family members in Europe. Jonas Marx, a prominent Jerusalem resident, took up the cause of one of the jailed men, named Weiner. He wrote Ruppin a strongly worded letter urging him to resolve the case as quickly as possible, no matter the expense. "I have visited young Mr. Weiner in prison, I will tell you openly that I consider his health to be quite at risk," Marx wrote. "It seems to me that he was probably used to a great deal of movement and is now unhealthily bloated from only sitting still."

Not only the man's life was at stake, Marx went on, but the good name of the colony, which was suffering from its being drawn into a murder case. "It certainly harms the reputation of the colony if it is seemingly not powerful enough to free one of their own, a man who is certainly innocent, from a situation that is not only dishonorable but dangerous to his health." Rebecka Weiner, the accused murderer's sister, also kept up a steady correspondence with Ruppin. When her brother was transferred to the central prison, where he was kept with other criminal defendants awaiting trial, she was aghast. "At the moment, my brother is in the same prison in one room with 350 Arabs," she wrote to Ruppin, adding, "and what kind of people are they?"

Zarnuqa was also struggling with repercussions from the recent events. A military post had been set up outside it to maintain quiet, and some of its leading inhabitants had been arrested as suspects in the murder of the Jewish guard. Others had fled and gone into hiding, causing further disruptions. The report to the Zionist committee in Berlin stated that Zarnuqa's leaders had suggested that the two sides resolve their dispute privately and not involve the government, a suggestion the report endorsed, concluding, "The colony also finds it better to begin such negotiations in a peaceful manner, so that the neighboring village will not become an enemy."

This was where Albert Antebi had become involved, having been retained by the Zionists to broker a peaceful resolution. Antebi had agreed to help immediately, throwing himself into sessions with the Zionists and their lawyers to plot strategy, meeting with the governor of Jerusalem regularly to apprise him of the situation and to sound him out on the feasibility of various possible compromises, and trying to ensure that Weiner's time in prison would not be too harsh, writing him and bringing him food on his visits. But he felt that everything about the case reflected the weaknesses of the Zionists, and their lack of understanding about how to get along with their neighbors.

For Antebi, the Rehovot incident had been the very thing he had warned might occur. Until then he had always believed that when it came to dividing "us" versus "them," the "us" were the Ottomans, Muslims, Christians, and Jews alike, who shared not only Jerusalem but the same history. Rehovot was one of the first significant blows to this notion—suddenly "us" became Jews and "them" Arabs, or vice versa, depending on where you stood. When Antebi examined the circumstances that led up to the confrontation at Rehovot, he realized that as much as he disliked the Zionists and their methods, if forced to choose, he knew which side he would take, and it was with the Jews.

He concluded that it probably should not have come as a surprise that the Jewish settlers at Rehovot and the Arab villagers who lived nearby in the village of Zarnuqa should have ended up in conflict. From the onset of the establishment of Jewish settlements in Palestine in the 1880s, confrontations over the land had been increasingly frequent, but tensions usually eased after the villagers were allowed to lease back some of the land that the settlement had bought or were hired to work on parts of their former properties.

But this existing arrangement was undone when Arthur Ruppin's Palestine Office not only acquired more land for settlement but hired only Jewish laborers to farm it. In a speech that he gave at the 1913 Zionist Congress in Vienna Ruppin had insisted that the new policy had nothing to do with Jewish animosity toward Arabs. Rather, he and many other Zionist leaders shared an almost mystical belief that unless Jews worked the land themselves, accepting no help from the Arab villagers who lived next to them, then the land did not truly belong to them.

After the implementation of the "Hebrew labor only" policy, violence was almost inevitable. When surveyors turned up to measure the newly acquired Jewish properties, they were frequently shot at or chased away by angry Arab villagers. In 1909, in response to the mounting attacks and the lack of government support on the ground in Palestine for Jewish colonization efforts, the organization HaShomer, or "The Guardian," a paramilitary group, was established.

In 1913, HaShomer was at the height of its powers, with responsibility for guarding virtually all of the largest, most established and important Jewish settlements in Palestine, including Rehovot. The group used its new power to pressure the settlements to fire any Arab laborers who remained and hire only Jewish ones, in some cases even making this a condition for taking on guard duties. In instances where the settlements refused to comply, either because of personal relationships with some of the Arab workers or due to financial constraints, then HaShomer implemented tougher security measures that often resulted in the further separation of Arab and Jewish workers. In Rehovot, a curfew was instituted by the HaShomer guards, so that Arab workers who did not return to their villages at night because they had early-morning chores and slept in the cowsheds were now instructed to shut the settlement's gates behind them, which were then locked.

Antebi had always thought that, like hiring only Jewish laborers, employing only Jewish guards was a bad idea. Settlements that used HaShomer saw their security expenses skyrocket because the Jewish guards charged so much more than Arab ones. In Rehovot, the settlement went from spending 11,000 francs on security to 18,000 francs in a single year after HaShomer took over guard duty. At first, no one questioned the added costs, as having HaShomer protection tapped into a sense of Jewish pride that seemed to infect everyone.

Antebi dismissed the Palestine Office's proposal of conducting negotiations with Zarnuqa as a bad idea. The time for moderation had been before the murder, not now. He reiterated his concerns about the "Hebrew labor only" policy, and stressed that it would be more productive, in the wake of what had happened in Rehovot, that if only Jewish guards were going to be used, then at least they should be natives of Palestine and able to speak Arabic. The new immigrants from Russia who formed the bulk of the population of settlers as well as filled HaShomer's ranks were either "hotheads," as Antebi described them, or like the Rehovot guard who had been killed: untrained, an easy mark for anyone with a gun, with no hope of being "able to dream of defending himself," as Antebi pointed out.

As far as Antebi was concerned, the lack of knowledge about how to deal with the Arabs had been one of the causes of the problem in the first place, and now threatened to make matters worse. "The brawl itself [over the grapes] was useless," he recounted in a letter back to his employers in Paris about the situation. Why hadn't the Jewish guards waited until the merchandise in the cart had been delivered to Rehovot, and then in a calm manner and at a later time brought their complaints to Zarnuqa's elders about the theft of the grapes? Why had they provoked a fight in the middle of the road, where each side could bring in reinforcements and escalate what was essentially a small dispute into a violent, full-blown confrontation?

Given that the Zionists' obstinacy and refusal to take advice from people who knew the Arabs had created the very conditions that gave rise to the current troubles, Antebi was shocked that they were already talking of making peace "before judicially establishing the aggression of Muslims against us."

The villagers of Zarnuqa had filed an official complaint with the authorities against the guards employed by the Jewish colonies. The village heads maintained that the guards "kill, pillage and rape Muslim women and girls." They called for the expulsion of any guard who was not formally registered with the Ottoman government, a provision that, if strictly enforced, would be a blow to the

Jewish colonies' manpower, since most of their inhabitants were not officially registered anywhere as residents of Palestine.

When Antebi heard these terrible accusations, he was adamant that they be forcefully countered before any peace talks between the two villages get under way. He warned the Zionist leaders that Ottoman politicians like Ruhi Khalidi were looking for any reason to oppose and stop Jewish immigration, land-buying, and settlement in Palestine, and that the situation, if not handled judiciously, could provide just such an excuse. But not only colonization was at stake, Antebi realized—so was the way history would be written. If the complaints were not vigorously fought, if the Muslim role in the violence was not formally established and publicly acknowledged, then "tomorrow the story of the wolf will be applied to us," he wrote, "our complaints will not be believed, and public rumor, well-formed by our adversaries, will accuse the Jews of a systematic persecution of the farmers."

As it happened, Antebi did not have to wait long to see his predictions borne out, for "the story of the wolf" circulated in Jerusalem all that summer. At the same time that he bribed jail officials to look after Weiner's well-being and met with the governor of Jerusalem to present his own petition outlining grievances of the Jewish colonies countering the charges made against them by their Arab neighbors, he also kept track of how events played out in the Jerusalem cafés, in the newspapers, and in the general gossip. The court of public opinion was one that Antebi understood and respected, and he feared that the Jews were losing there.

Eventually, the dispute with Zarnuqa was resolved after a fashion. Money was paid to compensate the family of the murdered villager, Weiner was released from jail, and Antebi led a delegation to an important religious official in Hebron, who helped broker a formal reconciliation between Zarnuqa and Rehovot. While peace was officially reestablished between the two communities, the affair lived on, dragging down people in its wake. Soon after, HaShomer lost its contract with Rehovot, whose leaders quietly went back to employing both Jewish and Arab guards.

The coverage that appeared about the conflict in the local press was all too indicative of the tensions in the region, as the parties involved could not even agree on the basic facts about the incident. David Moyal, who had served as the lawyer for Rehovot in the case, wrote an article in the Arabic-language paper *Filastin* that he called "A Word of Truth for the Sake of Peace." Moyal protested that the account of the conflict that had appeared in the paper was "intended to bring strife to brothers who, with regard to citizenship, interests, and the future, are similar. . . . I am sure my Islamic brothers do not share the feelings of the [article's] author."

In Moyal's recounting of the facts, Arabs from Zarnuqa had come into the vineyards owned by Rehovot to steal grapes. When the Jewish guard confronted them, they hit him and took his gun. The other guards gave chase, but by this time inaccurate rumors had gotten back to Zarnuqa that some Jews had killed an Arab. Enraged farmers hurried to the scene, and the Jewish guards were now confronted by a mob. "The situation was such that the Arabs believed that the Jews had killed a Muslim and the Jews saw that they wanted to take action against them," Moyal wrote.

A Jewish farmer who happened to be in Zarnuqa at the time acted as an intermediary between the guards and the angry mob and tried to stop the fighting. He was backed up by a Muslim sheik whom he had been visiting, who also urged the crowd to disperse. No one had been killed, the two men assured the crowd; the issue concerned a dispute over grapes, and now it was over. People began to heed their advice, until, Moyal wrote, one Muslim in the crowd suddenly, and with no provocation, drew his sword from its scabbard and started screaming, "Pig, son of a dog."

The sight of the man waving a sword and screaming insults caused the fighting to break out again, and in the confusion that followed, one of the Arab villagers was fatally shot. "The Jews did not begin the fight," Moyal summed up, "the Jews wanted to come to an understanding with the Arabs in a peaceful and accommodating manner, not with the sword and the revolver, the fellahs and not the Jews started the shooting."

In August 1913, a response to Moyal's article appeared in *Filastin*. Moyal, and by extension the Zionists whom he represented, wanted to place the blame for the violence on the Arabs, the writer stated, when in fact it all had been initiated by the Jews. "I say that these Jews came to our land as guests," the author wrote, "and when they saw that they could live with us, then they thought that we and our government were weak and they wanted to chase us out of our land. If one of us wants to insist on his rights, then they try to do everything bad to him in different ways and they pretend as if they love peace and all humanity." The villagers in Zarnuqa had their own grapes, the article observed, and would therefore hardly endanger themselves by stealing from the Jews what they already possessed in abundance. Likewise, they would never dare to hit a guard and steal his gun, because they were well aware of the seriousness of the consequences of such a theft.

"The pure truth is that a driver from Zarnuqa, who had grapes in his wagon, met two farmers from his village and gave them some grapes, as is the Arab custom," the author wrote. As the farmers sat together and ate at the side of the road, a Jewish guard approached them and wrongly accused them of stealing the grapes from the vineyards belonging to Rehovot. "He would not believe their words and did not want to listen to their pleas," the article continued. And because the farmers could not get away from the guard and he continued to accuse them of lying, they hit him and took away his weapon—otherwise, they feared, they would be shot and killed for something that they had not even done. "If they had really meant the Jews harm," the writer argued, "they would have killed the guard."

But when other Jews heard the shouting and gave chase, the Muslim farmers who dropped their tools in the fields and came running over to help their neighbors had had no other choice. Their only intention was to save their humiliated brothers, the author concluded. "When we see that a [Jewish] colony hurries to help another," he wrote, "is it any wonder that one Arab helps another in his need?"

One could not see those two articles side by side without realizing that Rehovot was not some aberration, "a sad incident," as the official report had put it, but the face of things to come. The outlines of a bloody conflict had by now clearly emerged. Antebi had written after everything happened at Rehovot that the incident had been "a hard lesson" for the Zionists. But when he read the final words in the *Filastin* article, he must have realized that the Jews were not the only ones who had learned a lesson.

4

Throughout 1913 the violence only continued all around Palestine. Within the Old City, the heart of Jerusalem, life at first seemed to go on much as it always had. Homes were still stocked with flour and chickpeas, green beans and cracked wheat, lentils and spaghetti, olives and cheese, awaiting any guest who turned up unexpectedly wanting to share the afternoon meal. On the rooftops large metal cages filled with pigeons were turned toward the east so the birds could enjoy the Jerusalem sun. Pairs of pigeons could be seen flying around the city all day long before returning to their sanctuaries for food and drink, their cooing blending in with the cacophony of the city's streets.

In the courtyards of the apartment buildings, women stood in the sun, bending to hang their laundry on the lines that were strung up, neighbors' towels and wet clothing drying in the mild afternoon air. The children sat, hunched on their knees, about to tip over, whiling away the time playing games, staring at piles of cards or marbles or jacks. Sometimes they borrowed an older relative's backgammon set and competed against one another, shaking the dice inside the cup with a furtive glance at their mothers to see if they noticed that they were betting small sums of money. Older men and a few younger ones who could not find jobs sat outside smoking water pipes, gossiping and chatting, passing the day's newspaper around between them. And there was always a young child who could be counted on to find a board and set up a seesaw in the yard, his friends all pushing to take a turn on the makeshift attraction.

The smell of baking often filled the courtyard, and the children jostled in anticipation, because the unspoken rule was that if you were baking and your neighbor could smell what was cooking—and in these closed quarters, with the windows open trying to catch a breeze, it was rare that aromas from the local ovens would not waft through the streets—then a portion of whatever was being prepared was sent over, so that every neighbor could share in the other's good fortune. In this way, even when people did not sit down together formally at a meal, they were in a real sense always guests at their neighbors' tables.

Even in the face of the news from Rehovot the rituals that had always bound Jerusalem's neighborhoods together seemed to be holding. During Ramadan, the monthlong fast, that year every evening at sunset a cannon would sound to announce the end of the day's fasting, its report seeming to shake the very walls of the city. The cannon was the signal for all the children of the neighborhood to gather in the courtyard with their instruments—flutes and recorders, cymbals, a small oud, even a stick to bang against a pot—

and make their way down the street, playing and singing, stopping at each neighbor's house to demand sweets.

In the market, the merchants sat patiently waiting for the same signal to allow them to start selling their wares, each inch of their space preciously guarded so that a rival might not encroach upon it. After the evening meal the women would occasionally steal away for a few moments to the roof, sitting like flowers with their heads covered in scarves, watching the tide of the city flow below them, calling out from time to time to one of their children or a neighbor's child who passed by or who seemed to be getting into trouble and needed a sharp word of discipline.

Jerusalem had not been cut off completely from the turmoil dividing the country that year. It had experienced one aspect of that conflict in the controversy over the rival Masonic lodges. But developments in the wider culture had also inexorably seeped in and slowly started to transform daily life in the city.

Now, for just one Ottoman *bishlik* paid at the door of many of the city's coffee shops, you could enter a darkened area and watch moving pictures being screened from a projector. The city's first automobile, driven by an American Christian who had come to Palestine, could be seen noisily making its way around town. Bakeries and some of the other shops had begun hiring actors at the cafés to sing, touting the wonderful goods for sale at the different areas around the Old City. There was now gambling in the back of some of the coffee shops.

It was not until November 1913 that the underlying tensions in Jerusalem finally exploded in what became known as the "language war."

When Herzl first began the Zionist movement, he had not envisioned Hebrew as the language of the future state. Because he himself couldn't speak it, it was automatically less appealing to him.

Likewise, the Zionist congresses' protocols were all written in German, as was much of the correspondence of Zionist officials. But by 1913, many Zionist leaders had come to value the potential of Hebrew as an instrument of nationalism.

Arthur Ruppin, a native German speaker, had tried for years to master the language. S. Y. Agnon, the great Hebrew writer who eventually won a Nobel Prize in Literature, even moved into Ruppin's house in order to be available at odd hours to tutor him, but to no avail. Ruppin constantly fretted that he was setting a bad example by not speaking better Hebrew. Still, as he traveled to Jewish settlements, he realized that it had to be promoted as the official language of the Jews. If not, as he noted in one diary entry, there would be a constant rivalry in Palestine between the proponents of German, French, or Arabic. Hebrew was the only language that could turn a group of people from all over the world into one unified nation.

The mounting campaign to use Hebrew inevitably forced a discussion about the fate of Arabic at the new Jewish schools opening up all over Palestine. How much time during the school day should be spent teaching Arabic when so many Jews still did not even speak Hebrew? Should the curriculum focus on spoken Arabic, or on reading and writing, a more literary Arabic? Behind this debate lay a crucial issue: Were Jews going to speak Arabic just for their practical daily needs, or would they learn the language in order to see themselves as part of a broader Arabic culture?

In the spring of 1913 the Association of Hebrew Teachers of Arabic, a professional group composed mainly of Jews who had grown up in Palestine or other parts of the Ottoman Empire, met in Jaffa to debate what position they should take on Arabic's future among the Jews. Nissim Malul, one of the attendees, urged the association to take a strong stand on teaching Arabic, which he and his supporters believed could help to change the direction of the emerging conflict with the Arabs. The majority in the group rejected that position, however, arguing, "We are teachers and we need to talk about Arabic instruction."

Malul then took his own case for Arabic to the papers. In June 1913, a three-part series appeared in *HaHerut* that stated that without Arabic, the Jews would effectively become an island in the region. "If we desire to root ourselves here in the mode of the land of the past and of the future," Malul wrote, "then we must learn the language of the land and think in it more than compared to other languages."

Malul's paean to Arabic did not win him many adherents. The editor of *HaHerut* wrote an opposing editorial in which he argued that learning Arabic was indeed important, but that Hebrew was the key to the rising Jewish national renaissance.

Then, in November 1913, the simmering debates about language came to a head. The Laemel School had opened in Jerusalem in 1903, sponsored by a German group. Its principal, Ephraim Cohen-Reiss, had decided that Hebrew should be taught there, and the school's auditorium had been the venue for the first play performed in Hebrew in Palestine, Israel Zangwill's *Zerubquel*.

But when the same German group decided to open a technical school in Haifa, to be called the Technion, its board of governors declared that instruction would be given in German, not Hebrew. Cohen-Reiss agreed with that decision, in the belief that modern Hebrew still lacked sufficient technical terms to allow for instruction in specialized disciplines. The Zionists, in turn, proposed a compromise: all schools in Palestine would use Hebrew for instruction, but at the Technion, German would be the preferred language, except in one science course that would be taught in Hebrew. When the Germans rejected this proposal, teachers at the Laemel School asked Cohen-Reiss to adopt Hebrew in all the schools under his jurisdiction in the city, as a sign of support for the Zionists at the Technion. He refused.

In December 1913, a group of students and teachers marched through the streets of Jerusalem to the Laemel School, where they demonstrated in favor of using Hebrew exclusively in instruction. As the crowd grew angrier and angrier, someone threw a rock, and windows were broken. Cohen-Reiss, fearing the potential for even greater violence, called the police, who had to break up the demonstration. When the outraged teachers responded by going on strike, the students followed them out the doors in support. Many transferred to new Hebrew schools that had begun opening.

Eventually, the Germans backed down, and Hebrew became the language of instruction even at the Technion. Nissim Malul's fight for Arabic had ended as well, and *Filastin* reported ominously that the victory for Hebrew in the "language war" was a sign of Zionism's ascendancy. Hebrew was a language that was "useless to the world," the editorial went on, "except as a weapon of Zionism."

5

Amid the growing violence in Palestine the Zionist Congress assembled for its annual meeting in September 1913 in Vienna. Arthur Ruppin was scheduled to deliver a lecture, and despite the private Hebrew lessons, he spoke in German. Before arriving in Vienna, Ruppin had spent several weeks with his daughter, Ruth, working on his speech for the Congress. "To this day," he later commented, "I consider that talk the best I ever gave."

The Congress had met ten times prior to 1913, including in Basel, London, The Hague, and Hamburg. The gathering in Vienna, Herzl's city of birth, would be the last major Zionist convention before the outbreak of World War I, and also the largest.

By now the meeting had become far more than a mere political gathering. It was the de facto center of Zionist culture, setting the agenda as well as the fashion for the coming year. Here delegates could drink wine from grapes grown in one of the many Jewish settlements in Palestine. The men wore pins in their lapels with the Zionist flag Herzl had designed, and brought back extras for friends at home who had been unable to attend the Congress. Concerts were held at which symphonic versions of Hebrew songs were played by orchestras, and Jewish athletes put on sports shows, grunting in Hebrew. Various slide shows and a movie documented Jewish pioneers at work on the land.

In some ways, the 1913 Congress represented a referendum on the future of the work in Palestine. The reports of violent clashes with the Arabs, despite being played down by Ruppin and others in the Palestine Office, had alarmed many of the European members. At the same time, some of the Zionists' showpiece projects, like the Bezalel art school in Jerusalem, were subjected to scathing criticism by the delegates, who wondered if their money was being spent wisely on such endeavors.

To some attending the Congress, the news that Bezalel was struggling to remain open was symbolic of the entire Zionist enterprise in Palestine: heartwarming, emotionally inspiring, but ultimately impractical and not viable financially. David Tolkowski, one of the delegates, criticized the Jewish workers for demanding higher salaries, which raised the costs of the settlement movement. "They import expensive herring to make borscht," he lamented, recommending that they switch to the less expensive and more healthful bean soups and polenta for their meals.

There were many attendees who tried to answer the critics. Chaim Weizmann, who later became the first president of the modern state of Israel, was willing to concede the truth of all the points at issue—that the settlements didn't make money yet, that Bezalel art school was "a losing proposition," even that polenta and bean soup were better to eat than borscht, if conceding that would appease the critics. But he urged the delegates to recognize one significant fact: that their power lay in the ownership of land in Palestine. "Do you think anyone would talk to us at all seriously if you just spoke at congresses in Vienna or The Hague?" he asked. "The political persuasiveness [of the Zionists] will grow proportionately to our position in Palestine."

In his own speech Ruppin argued that Bezalel, the settlements, and all the other projects in Palestine had been in service of one main idea—the desire, he said, "to create in Palestine a Jewish community with its own culture." But over the past year, what the violence and the clashes had taught them was that in order to sustain such a culture, "the Jewish population will have to be in the majority." For this to happen, Ruppin stated, "we will therefore have to acquire the greater part of the land in Palestine."

Other speakers proposed an additional way to further strengthen and perhaps even deepen the Jewish hold on Palestine: through Jerusalem itself.

Jerusalem had never figured all that prominently in the Zionist liturgy, at least not before 1913. Herzl had set his novel about the future of Palestine in Haifa, believing the future of the Zionist movement lay there. Ruppin first opened the Palestine Office in Jaffa, which was also the site of the office of the Anglo-Palestine Company, the Zionist bank that put together the financing for most of the land purchases in the country; the agency for the Odessa Committee, which was part of Hovevei Zion, the Russian Jewish group that had sent some of the first Jewish settlers to Palestine; and of Geulah, another Jewish land-buying corporation.

But at the 1913 Zionist Congress, Jerusalem's name was on everyone's lips. There was discussion about how to more rapidly build the new Jewish culture in Palestine, and when talk turned to the plans for a national library, a national archaeological museum, and a national university, it was the only city considered for the location of all these institutions.

If the Zionists intended to pursue Ruppin's idea of trying to become a majority in Palestine, to focus on gaining control of more land and creating a broad base from which Jewish culture could thrive, it was apparent that Jerusalem had to be the focus. It was the only city in Palestine that could unite the passions of Jews all over the world. To purchase the amount of land that Ruppin envisioned, a mammoth fund-raising operation would be required, and no city but Jerusalem could inspire such generous donations from around the world.

Menachem Ussishkin, who had once participated in the walkout at a Zionist Congress when Herzl proposed establishing a homeland somewhere other than Palestine, also extolled the merits of Jerusalem, after complaining that the city had been neglected. "Years ago, when we started colonizing Palestine, the opinion was spread around that Jerusalem was too rotten, too impossible, for a modern culture, and the new settlements were concentrated around Jaffa," he told the delegates. "Now it is getting its revenge: Jerusalem is perishing. . . . We must and shall tie our work to Jerusalem," he urged, "as Palestine's and Jewish national feelings' natural center."

Ussishkin brought the audience to its feet when he reminded it that twenty-five hundred years earlier, the First Temple in Jerusalem had been destroyed by the Babylonian army, the city razed, the people scattered, and the empire of the Israelites had come to a crashing end. And now, he told the delegates, they—the inheritors of this amazing legacy—had the honor of considering resurrecting "a temple of culture and learning on Mount Zion" in their push to found a national university in Jerusalem. "Today we stand ready to breathe life into a courageous plan," he announced.

Chaim Weizmann also expounded on that theme, explaining how

the idea of a university in Jerusalem had long been a cherished project but had been set aside because of more urgent matters. But now the timing was right to revive the plan. In fact, he insisted, it was critical that a national university in Jerusalem be founded as a symbol of Jewish renewal, which would further be promoted by its offering courses taught in Hebrew. The vision of a Jewish university in Jerusalem inspired a kind of poetry in people's speeches, a level of grandiosity that somehow all the talk of banks and settlements and land deals failed to elicit. It enabled the delegates to draw the connection between Jewish power in Jerusalem and Ruppin's grand vision for Palestine. It all seemed within reach.

Once the idea of the university was raised, it seemed as if the energy could not be contained. "We are approaching our goal," one delegate stood up and declared. "We are approaching the goal of a new shrine on Mount Zion again." Another delegate, Boris Goldberg, suggested establishing a special arm of Ruppin's Palestine Office to focus solely on developing industry and trade in Jerusalem. A Dr. Friedemann noted that "Jewish antiquities have been lost for 2,000 years," but thanks to archaeological digging under way in Jerusalem, they were now being recovered and collected. A museum should be set up in Jerusalem to house these tangible reminders of Jewish power in the past and its continuing presence in the city.

When the conference finally ended after four days, the delegates scattered to spread the new doctrine of Jerusalem. Back in Russia, Menachem Ussishkin spoke eloquently about the city as "the heart of the nation and the world" in speeches that were printed and circulated not only in Russia but in Palestine as well. He called for a stronger Jerusalem, a muscular Jerusalem, one "surrounded by a ring of Jewish settlements." He urged the removal of the dirt and debris from the Wailing Wall, the only remnant of the temples that had once stood in Jerusalem, and its reclamation as a symbol of the Jewish renaissance. The true goal of Zionism, he argued—and it was an argument that could not have been easily made or fallen on such receptive ears without the groundwork laid at the 1913 Congress—was "a New Jerusalem, a Jerusalem of which a truly cultural nation can indeed be proud."

A New Jerusalem—this was the image they had been searching for, the rallying cry that would put to rest the petty squabbling, the debates over herring or polenta, the personal rivalries, the ego and self-aggrandizement that marks all political movements and could have strangled Zionism before it was able to truly establish secure roots in Palestine.

Tens of thousands of poor Russians, inspired by the call issued at the Zionist Congress, dug into their pockets and sent 50,000 gold francs to the Palestine Office's coffers. This degree of generosity from the Jewish masses did not go unnoticed by Zionist leaders. Six months after the Congress, armed with a sum of money he never anticipated, and galvanized by a vision that he knew could help him achieve the goals he had set out in his speech in Vienna, Arthur Ruppin wrote, "Today I succeeded in buying from Sir John Gray Hill his large and magnificently situated property on Mount Scopus, thus acquiring the first piece of ground for the Jewish university in Jerusalem."

Less than a week after Ruppin's fortunate purchase on Mount Scopus, the British consul in the city wrote to his superiors that it seemed to him that in Jerusalem "a Jewish nationalist spirit" was on the rise.

6

What many in the audience at the Zionist Congress in 1913 did not know was that even as he sat patiently through the endless meetings in Vienna, Victor Jacobson was overseeing a series of secret negotiations between the Zionists and leading Arab nationalists in the hope of reaching some kind of agreement before the violence and the growing conflict spun completely out of control.

Jacobson's mission was too sensitive, and its outcome too uncertain, to allow it to become part of the public discourse. No one wanted to open up the delicate negotiations to the scrutiny of the Zionist rank and file. So Jacobson said nothing that week about the topic that would come to dominate the future of Palestine: How could Arabs and Jews coexist peacefully?

For someone like Jacobson, who was forty-three in 1913 and still vigorous and energetic, keeping silent about so important an issue wasn't easy. He was a good listener, a convivial dinner companion, a connoisseur who loved music and wine and good food. Along with his friend Weizmann and his brother-in-law Ussishkin, he had been one of twenty students who helped found a Russian Jewish scientific society that joined the Zionist movement shortly after its inception. Jacobson had argued with Herzl about its future and the proper direction it should take almost from the start.

The men in this scientific society eventually came to dominate the Zionist movement. After the Young Turks' coup in 1908, Jacobson had been tapped by the Zionist leadership to go set up an office in Constantinople, officially as the head of the Anglo-Palestine Bank branch there—the Zionist movement's financial arm—but actually as the Zionists' main representative in the capital.

As part of his job, Jacobson cultivated Ottoman officials, met with Palestinian delegates to the newly established Parliament, and tried to raise the profile of the Zionist movement among Constantinople's large Jewish population. He was also the source of much of the Zionist largesse in the city, putting many newspaper editors on the Zionist payroll in exchange for printing news or positive mentions of the Zionist program in Palestine, and doling out the necessary bribes to smooth the Zionists' way into the offices of Ottoman officials who might help them purchase more land.

Jacobson was known for his large dinner parties, where he might make a gracious toast in French or German as easily as in his native Russian. But he also had a keen political eye, good judgment, and sharp instincts. After he heard Ruhi Khalidi's famous 1911 speech decrying Zionism, Jewish immigration, and land purchases in Palestine, he sent Ussishkin a note in which he predicted that the speech's sentiments were no aberration and that from now on the Zionists would have to maneuver within and live from "storm to storm."

Later, he would write numerous frank reports about the obstacles to making peace with the Arabs. In one letter to Arthur Ruppin, he recounted how he had been in contact or met with any number of individuals, all of whom identified themselves as the leaders of various Arab groups. "Each one claims that it is he who is the real, the only real, the important one," he complained. "There is no way of knowing what truth there is in what they say, what is behind them."

Still, this did not stop him from moving forward and trying to find a path that would benefit the Zionists. Whenever the peace talks appeared to reach an impasse, he put forth any number of clever ideas that he hoped might bridge the two sides' positions. His subsequent assessments of why the Arabs and the Jews remained so far apart offer the best synopsis of how negotiations failed, and his insights remain as relevant for today's difficulties as they were back in 1913 when he was in charge of shepherding the first peace talks.

Jacobson had been brought into the negotiations by his friend Sami Hochberg, who was the editor of *Le Jeune Turc*, one of the Constantinople papers on the Zionists' payroll. Hochberg had come to Palestine from Bessarabia at the age of twenty in 1889, arriving with the first waves of Jewish immigrants. He soon became involved with virtually every aspect of the Zionist experience there, working as a farmer and a watchman at Rishon LeZion, establishing with a small group of workers another settlement in Nes Tzionna, and teaching Arabic to Jewish settlers. But he remained a man who felt

at home anywhere in the Ottoman Empire. Hochberg was precisely
the kind of connected individual Jacobson was eager to tap in Constantinople. As a go-between to the Arabs, he had another point in his
favor: since he was neither an official employee nor a high-ranking
member of the Zionist movement like Jacobson, his mission could
be disavowed at any time with few political repercussions to the
Zionists.

The first initiative for the 1913 negotiations came from the Arabs,
in particular from a group that had founded the Decentralization
Party in Egypt to seek political autonomy for Arabs within the Ottoman Empire. In articles that appeared in the Arabic press in 1913,
members of this group argued that the Zionist movement was making a mistake in trying to court Ottoman officials to sanction their
program in Palestine without first coming to terms with local Palestinians. "Without the consent of . . . Arabs . . . , enmity against the
Jews will be reborn today, an enmity which will fight with all possible
means against the interests of Zionism in order to annul the accom-
plished work and to drain from it all hope for the future," one of the
editorials stated. The writer called on the Zionist leaders "to consider friendship with their close neighbor, which is preferable to that
of the far away foreigner." In a postscript, the editor added, "It is
imperative that an entente between Zionists and Arabs be made because a war of words can only do harm."

Jacobson sent Hochberg to Cairo to meet with the leaders of the
Decentralization Party, to identify common ground, and to determine if there was a chance of reaching an agreement. Hochberg
ultimately met with members of various political parties interested
in reform while he was there.

Hochberg sent back a report on what he called "The Arab Movement" that Jacobson read repeatedly and that was circulated widely
among the top Zionist leadership. It chronicled the emergence of an
Arab national movement and the urgent need for Zionists to find a

way to understand, address, and deal with it. Hochberg argued that although Arab nationalism had a long history, it had only recently changed from "being an idea and a desire to being an action in hopes of realization." When the Young Turks came to power, the Arabs had hoped they would now be free to develop their own culture within the context of a broader Ottoman identity. But the promised reforms were slow in coming, and much of their hopes for genuine change were dashed.

The Balkan Wars, the loss of many of the empire's outer provinces, and the continuing political turmoil in Constantinople that this loss caused led the Arab nationalists to reach a critical conclusion, Hochberg's report observed: the Ottoman Empire was weak, unable to defend itself from strong nationalist movements that might take up arms against it. "This is therefore the beginning of the end," Hochberg said the intellectuals and activists with whom he met in Cairo explained to him. These men, he added, "thought it [their] duty as Arabs and as Muslims to sound the cry of alarm while there is still time to save the Arab provinces from the destructive fire which is throwing its flaming tongues in all directions of the Empire." These same thinkers had concluded that they might find common cause with the Zionists, in the hope of forcing the government to grant all of them greater autonomy over their own communities.

Hochberg told Jacobson that an Arab-Syrian Congress planned for June 1913 in Paris would be "the first step made by the Arab movement to go from theory to practice, from dreams to action." He felt it was imperative that a Zionist representative attend, because in Paris, "the Arab movement will take shape." That movement, Hochberg wrote in his memo, "is much more serious than it is imagined in Constantinople." He urged the Zionists to open up formal negotiations with the Arabs immediately, led by officials like Jacobson rather than go-betweens like himself.

The urgent question was whether it was possible to reach an

agreement now, before anyone embraced the idea of resolving the conflict over Palestine through the use of arms. "There is a means of finding common ground for an entente between this movement and Zionism," Hochberg stated in his report. "We must influence them in our favor from the very beginning in order to not give time to our adversaries to influence them against us."

Opening ceremonies for the Congress were held at the auditorium of the French Geographical Society at 2:30 p.m. on June 24, 1913. There were 150 observers gathered that day, but only a total of 23 official delegates who actually participated, including 11 Muslims, 11 Christians, and 1 Jew—Sami Hochberg. Jacobson had given Hochberg a 2,000-franc budget to take his Arab counterparts to dinner while he was there, which Hochberg put to good use, hosting a dinner for the key representatives the night before they were scheduled to debate the issue of immigration to Palestine. He hoped to impress on them his point that the Arabs had nothing to fear and no reason to oppose the further influx of Jewish immigrants.

Still, the growing conflict between Jews and Arabs in Palestine was a relatively minor issue at the Congress, where the delegates were focused much more on securing increased power for Arabs throughout the empire. At the end, the delegates passed a series of resolutions that summed up their key demands. They wanted Arabic to be considered an official language in Arab-dominated parts of the empire, and to be recognized in Parliament. Arab men conscripted for military service should be allowed to fulfill their obligation in their local villages, rather than being sent to remote corners of the empire where they knew no one.

Many of their demands had much common ground with the direction the Zionists were pursuing for themselves in Palestine, and even this most tentative beginning of negotiations between the Arabs and the Jews over the future of Palestine did not go unnoticed in Constantinople. Officials there decided to send their own representatives to Paris to try to make a deal with the Arab nationalists before Hochberg or Jacobson had a chance to conclude one of their own. After the Congress ended, the Ottoman government signed an agreement with the Arab leaders that granted them some of their most important points. Under its terms, the Ottomans conceded that in countries where the majority of the population was Arab, Arabic would be the language in the schools, and that Turkish-appointed officials would have to be Arabic speakers.

But by the time the agreements' terms were publicly disseminated two months later, many of the various concessions had been watered down by officials who read them and changed their provisions. The final agreement was viewed as a disappointment by many Arab political leaders, who felt they had been promised more during the heady days of the meetings in Paris than was eventually delivered.

Still, the signed agreement gave the Arabs a more influential position in terms of dictating the future direction of Palestine, which only increased the urgency of Zionists' coming to terms with them. By October 1913, Jacobson would write in a letter to a Zionist backer, "The first article of our work program ought to be an entente with the Arabs."

By the beginning of 1914 Jacobson was working hard to make this a reality by organizing an official meeting. Ruhi Khalidi's cousin in Jerusalem, Nasif Khalidi, contacted Jacobson offering to act as an intermediary. Nasif Khalidi was a civil engineer by trade, and had served on the same public works committee in Jerusalem as Albert Antebi, trying to develop projects to improve the infrastructure of the city. By 1914, he had been appointed the chief engineer in Beirut. When Nahum Sokolow, a Zionist leader, came to Beirut on a tour of the region, it was Khalidi who arranged for him to meet a number of Arab leaders.

During Sokolow's visit, Jacobson did what he knew best—he threw a dinner party, where he worked the room and tried to enlist

Sami Bakr, the governor of Beirut, as an ally. Later, Jacobson recorded that the governor had not been adamantly opposed to increasing Jewish immigration to Palestine, as long as the new arrivals agreed to give up their original passports and to take on Ottoman citizenship. The governor had even come up with his own suggestions for fostering greater integration between the two sides, such as encouraging the Technion school to introduce Arabic-taught courses so that Arabs could attend it.

After Sokolow returned to Berlin, it became increasingly clear over the ensuing months that the more ambitious meeting Jacobson and Khalidi were trying to broker for later in the year would be more difficult to arrange than they had originally anticipated. Sending Sami Hochberg to Paris had posed relatively little risk because he was not a high-ranking member of the Zionist movement, and anything he said or agreed to could ultimately be disavowed if necessary. Now, however, each side hesitated at precisely the moment when decisive action and commitment was required. Jacobson had trouble getting the Zionists to come up with a list of potential delegates to the peace talks, as they wavered about sending representatives who were too high-ranking if the Arabs would not be willing or able to send a comparable delegation. Khalidi likewise encountered obstacles in compiling a list of Arab representatives, as the Arabs had their own conditions. They did not, for example, want to meet with any Zionists who had been deeply involved in land purchases in Palestine, which effectively ruled out virtually every Zionist leader who lived there.

Khalidi had also proposed an agenda for the meeting. The Arab delegates wanted the Zionists to clarify their aims in Palestine, particularly regarding the colonization of the land. After hearing their explanation, the Arabs would make their demands, Khalidi said. Only by the Zionists' acceptance of this condition, Khalidi told their representatives, would the Arabs be able to determine "whether the

[Zionist] movement could be considered harmful to the Arabs or not." Khalidi's position left many of the Zionist leaders fearing that a meeting might make matters worse, not better, for the Jews in Palestine.

In a 1914 memo summarizing the sputtering negotiations to date, Arthur Ruppin wrote that at the proposed conference, the Arabs "wanted to accuse us of forming separate settlements, in which we do not accept Arabs, namely in Tel Aviv and all the agricultural Jewish colonies. We have our own national hymn, national flag, our own court, yes even our own jail. Our schools are intended only for Jewish children; it is not enough to say that we have nothing against admitting Arab children in principle, but we must establish a curriculum and especially include Arabic instruction to such an extent that the schools would be suitable for Arab children as well."

Ruppin now started to wonder if "the participation on the side of the Arabs was not truly what we wish. . . . We could in no way be sure of an advantageous outcome" to peace talks, he wrote. "We would have rejected the Arabs' demands to move towards assimilation with the Arabs and would probably have received hardly any concessions of any consequence from them." The outcome, he surmised, could be a situation in which the Zionists "worsened [their] relationship to the Arabs instead of bettering it." His conclusion was that the Zionists should find a way to postpone the conference without causing such an outcome.

Other Zionist leaders shared Ruppin's judgment that postponement might be the best idea. Richard Lichtheim, who had arrived in Constantinople in 1914 to work with Jacobson, told his boss, "The Arabs are and will remain our natural opponents." What could the Zionists truly offer the Arabs, he added, other than a "promise to give all their demands serious consideration" and to "talk constantly of the necessity for both sides of a lasting agreement" without actually reaching one?

On the Arab side, those who had once favored an entente started to express their own reservations. Haqqi Bey al-Azm, one of the men who had met with Hochberg in Egypt in 1913, now wrote to one of his colleagues that while he was willing to talk to the Zionists, he felt the proposed meeting "has no purpose at all. . . . Understand, dear brother, that these people are marching towards their object at a rapid pace. I am sure that if we do nothing to affect the status quo, [the Zionists] will attain their object in a few years in [Palestine] where they will found [a Jewish state]."

In March 1914, another member of the group that had met with Hochberg in Cairo, Rashid Rida, wrote that there were only two possible courses of action open to the Arabs. The first was to make an agreement with the Zionists and settle their differences. If that failed, the Arabs must "gather all their forces to oppose the Zionists in every way." They would have to form "armed gangs," for above all, they must "oppose [the Zionists] by force."

Shortly after World War I commenced, plans for the conference that Jacobson had promoted were quietly abandoned. The organizers blamed the failed attempt on the difficulty of gathering so many people together during wartime. But by then, the issue was moot, for both the Zionists and the Arabs recognized that eventually there would be a parting of the ways. The only question that remained was how soon that would occur. Each side preferred to postpone the inevitable until a more advantageous moment.

PART FOUR

Jerusalem 1914

*On the eve of the war which became
the eve of all my wars . . .
And everything in three languages:
Hebrew, Arabic and Death.*

— YEHUDA AMICHAI

1

With the outbreak of World War I, Jerusalem became a city that felt increasingly claustrophobic to its inhabitants. For years it had been served by Austrian, German, French, and Italian post offices, where people could send letters or buy stamps, or simply speak another language with the clerk and those waiting in line. But with the onset of war they were closed down, until the sole survivor was the one run by the Ottomans, near the train station. That post office had been inefficient even during the best of times, with letters sent within Palestine taking weeks to arrive, if they got to their destination at all. The city began to feel cut off from the rest of the world, and even the whistle from the train that now arrived less often in Jerusalem seemed to blow forlornly.

During the summer of 1914 there was talk that for the first time, an airplane was to land in Jerusalem, along the road that led out of the city toward Bethlehem. The news of progress in technology appearing in Palestine was at first greeted with enthusiasm. Many people took it as a sign that the Ottoman government had not forsaken Jerusalem, and that with such displays of technical prowess it sought to demonstrate that the city could be defended. It seemed like the first sign of hope from the wide world outside the city's walls.

The day the plane was scheduled to touch down in Palestine was hot and dry, but people poured out of the city, headed toward the landing area. Women packed up their children, men shut their stores and abandoned their stations at the coffee shops, and by noon, Jerusalem was a ghost town. At first, the day had an air of festive celebration, despite the intense heat. People waited in excitement, straining to hear the sounds of an approaching engine. Some had brought flags to wave to welcome the pilots to the holy city of Jerusalem. But the afternoon drew on with no sign of the plane, and the heat grew more oppressive. Food and water ran low, and the crowd started to stir, restless, disappointed, hot, worried. Then suddenly news arrived—the airplane had crashed in the north of Palestine, near the city of Tiberias, killing its two pilots.

The news of the crash sent a chill through the crowd. Suddenly, as if trying to escape the approach of bad news, people packed up their belongings and started to disperse to make the long journey by foot back to Jerusalem. In the coffee shops that evening, the crash was interpreted as a bad omen, a sign of things to come for the city, and for Palestine. The Ottoman Empire's fate seemed as tenuous as that of the downed airplane, about to drop from the sky at any moment because it had attempted to fly too high.

The recent events had made Arthur Ruppin realize how vulnerable the Zionist movement's achievements also really were, how easily they, too, could be undermined by harsh reality. "Perhaps we are not strong enough for the gigantic task we have undertaken?" he wrote in his journal in 1914. "Will we be able to hold our own in the storms now shaking the country?"

The most disturbing news of all was that Ahmed Djemal, one of the three men now running the Ottoman Empire, had been given control of Jerusalem and was on his way to take charge of the city. It was clear that he regarded Jews as potential enemies of the state. In an article in *HaHerut*, he had given an interview in which he declared that the Zionists had already secretly formed their own government. "I have the honor of being the prime minister," Ruppin dryly noted in his journal. Ruppin realized that Djemal was a ruthless enemy who had the potential to destroy all the Zionists' achievements of the past years.

Shortly after his arrival in Jerusalem, Djemal implemented new rules that were designed to curtail the ability of the Zionists to continue their work. He forced Ruppin to give up his leadership of the Palestine Office in Jaffa and move to Jerusalem. He had wanted to exile Ruppin from Palestine entirely, but Ruppin promised the military officer that he would work on a book he had been hoping to write about the Syrian economy and stay out of politics. Apparently believing that his own contributions and achievements to the flowering of the Syrian economy would be the highlight of this work, Djemal gave his approval to the project and Ruppin's new focus and allowed him to stay in Palestine.

Ruppin did set to work on the book, but continued to try to salvage as much as he could from the situation without attracting too much attention to himself. All Zionist emblems—the Star of David, flags, the stamps picturing Herzl and Max Nordau that were used to raise money to help fund land purchases—had been banned by Djemal as emblems of nationalism and a separate, non-Ottoman identity. Djemal even accused Ruppin of high treason and had him brought before a Turkish court-martial in Jerusalem for a hearing that lasted five days. Ruppin had protested the inclusion of the Star of David—"I told them that they could find this symbol on the wall of the Old City in Jerusalem near the Damascus Gate," he explained to the judges, and although he was eventually acquitted, he could not convince anyone in the administration to see his point of view or to change Djemal's edict. Anyone found with any of these symbols on his person, in his home, or in his office, or caught displaying them at any public place would be banished from Palestine, the new leader of Jerusalem had declared.

Djemal also forced the Anglo-Palestine Bank, whose offices had helped spearhead the land drive by providing financing of all the purchases, to shut down and liquidate its assets. At the same time he ruled that all Jews who wanted to remain in Palestine must apply for Ottoman citizenship or face immediate deportation. But it cost one pound to become a citizen, money that most people did not have in wartime. Banks all over the country were closing their doors, and it was impossible to obtain or borrow money from family living outside the country. Virtually all lines of communication were destroyed or severely disrupted, most people had no idea what had become of their families back in Europe as the war raged. Assuming Ottoman citizenship presented other dilemmas, as well. "Many [Jews] did not dare to renounce their present nationality because according to the laws of their country they would be committing high treason," Ruppin wrote. No one knew which side would prevail in the conflict, and if they chose wrongly, they feared they might be killed as traitors at the war's end.

At one point, pleading the need to go to Syria in order to gather information for research, Ruppin managed to get to Damascus for a few days. There he saw Armenians wandering the city, homeless and broken, the victims of a persecution and a fate that he worried the Jews in Palestine would also suffer. Then in December 1914, his fears seemed to be borne out when five hundred Russian Jews were suddenly rounded up and ordered to be deported to Egypt by boat when they failed to show Ottoman identity cards to police.

"In vain I lodged a complaint," wrote Ruppin, but he no longer had any power or ability to influence the fate of the Jews for whom he felt responsible. The evening they were scheduled to be deported, he went down to the harbor in Jaffa to try to lend moral support and at the very least bear witness to what he feared would be the beginning of the end of the Zionist movement in Palestine. There he encountered a scene of frenzy, entire families hastily trying to collect all their belongings, counting heads, attempting to gather some food to take with them for the journey ahead.

"Old people, mothers with babies—being driven on to the boat in infinite disorder," Ruppin wrote about the scene he witnessed. Amid these images of despair, he realized that with only one order from

Djemal, a single decree or decision or edict, no Jew would be allowed to remain in Palestine, and all that the Zionists had managed to build so far would be destroyed, "the work of many years [gone] in a single day." How many trips had Ruppin taken, how many letters and pleas had he and others written, to convince those five hundred Jews to come to Palestine and settle there, to leave their homes and begin new lives? At the port, he handed out some money that he had been able to scrape together to help people on the way. But the scene, he wrote, "made me realize on what weak foundations our efforts at settlement rest."

It was not only the political situation that seemed grim, for Jerusalem was now beset by a debilitating series of woes. As Ruppin walked its streets, the citizens seemed like hunted animals, trying to stay hidden to avoid the blows that increasingly came without warning from every side. Some were due to the relentlessness of war. With so many men mobilized into the army, there weren't enough hands to bring in the crops. Even when labor was available, very few crops survived long enough to be worth the effort and the resources to harvest them. There was a shortage of fuel to run the irrigation pumps, so most crops did not get enough water. Entire fields turned brown, and in orchards the fruit shriveled and died on the vine while people starved back in the city. Sanitation had become virtually nonexistent. Jerusalem was overcrowded, dirty, and dependent on water that had to be brought from wells far away. Soon the city was hit by an epidemic of typhoid, but little help could be found for the ill. Most doctors and trained hospital personnel had been drafted into military service, and the supply shelves in hospitals had already been ransacked. By the end of the war, Palestine's Jewish population, once estimated at 85,000, had shrunk to 65,000 or less.

The Ottoman army, with its ill-fed and ill-equipped soldiers, was not faring any better than the general population. In an attempt to marshal its forces, it requisitioned anything it could get its hands on—farm animals, agricultural equipment, farm tools, foodstuffs that might have been stored away for hard times. At every level of society there was a sense that the entire world had turned against Jerusalem and Palestine.

In 1915 a plague of locusts swarmed the region. In his journal Ruppin recorded the sight of "airborne swarms of locusts [that] darkened the sky, the young ones, still unable to fly, crawled out of their eggs and formed processions 30 to 50 meters wide and several kilometers long and devoured the corn and the greenery on the trees." The country was literally being eaten alive. All around him, Ruppin saw signs of the growing devastation. Palestine's beauty was ravaged. "The branches in the orange groves [were] eaten away down to the white wood," Ruppin noted. They "stretched like skeletons into the air."

By now the people, too, had become little more than skeletons in the air, at the mercy of the elements and the whims of the country's leaders. At the beginning of 1915 Ahmed Djemal summoned thirty prominent Jewish leaders to the hotel where he was staying in Jerusalem, among them Arthur Ruppin and Albert Antebi. In recent years Antebi and Ruppin had grown close, each admiring the other's ability to get things done.

When the group arrived at the hotel at 4 p.m., the appointed time, they were told by a servant that Djemal was still in the bath. The men waited for an hour, speculating on why they had been summoned. Finally, the governor appeared, his hair still damp. He looked around at the assembly and abruptly announced, "You will all be deported to Brusa," a city in the mountains near the front lines of the war. Brusa (now known as Bursa) had been the first capital of the Ottoman Empire and still remained an important city. Then just as suddenly, Djemal left the room without another word.

The news was shocking, not just because of the disruption to their lives but because, as Ruppin recounted, "Deportation to Brusa in the winter, probably making most of the journey on foot, with typhoid everywhere, meant almost certain death."

The men debated their course of action, and decided to send Albert Antebi to speak on their behalf. Antebi knew Djemal from having worked with him since he first arrived in the city, and Antebi's wife regularly entertained the leader's wife, inviting her to tea as often as several times a week.

Antebi was gone for two hours, and his face was solemn when he returned to the hotel lobby where the men had been forced to wait for news of the verdict.

"An order which Djemal has given remains in force forever," he said gravely, recounting what he had been told when he first inquired about reversing the expulsions.

But after extensive discussions, Djemal had agreed to what Antebi called some "minor modifications." The Jews would still be deported, but to Tiberias, in northern Palestine. Their exile would not be permanent but only two weeks' duration. Finally, not all the original group would be obliged to leave. "So a few notables took a holiday in Tiberias," Ruppin summed up, "and the children of Israel were once more spared the decree."

2

One day in 1914, a few months after the war began, Wasif Jawhari-yyeh was walking from his family's house in the Old City when he saw "the first Arab hanged on a high gallows in a way that made everybody scared." The victim had on a white cloak. On his chest were written a number of words, perhaps an account of his crimes. Jawhariyyeh was too frightened to get close enough to read what they said. "This way, Jerusalem witnessed its first hanged Arab in a public way," he later wrote in his journal.

In the weeks that followed, Djemal had more and more Arab men executed, all of them hanged from trees directly outside the Jaffa Gate, the main entrance to the Old City. He ordered that their bodies remain suspended for days, so that anyone leaving or entering the city was forced to witness firsthand the result of opposing his rule.

The Arabs and Jews who had only recently fought over Jewish land purchases and Jewish immigration to Palestine now found themselves equally vulnerable to the dictates of the Ottomon leadership. Djemal considered all of them renegades, and he saw in the Arab-Jewish conflict what they themselves were finally starting to articulate: the beginning of a larger fight for control over the land of Palestine. From his perspective, it didn't matter which side won. Both groups threatened the continued dominance of Ottoman rule in Jerusalem, and so the military governor pursued both with a vengeance.

Entire families were deported. Arabic was banned, and once again Turkish became the official spoken language of public life. Abd Hamid al-Zahrawi, who in 1913 had met with Victor Jacobson and Sami Hochberg to discuss the possibility of a peace agreement between the Zionists and the Arabs during the Arab Congress in Paris, was executed. Shukri al-Asli, Ruhi Khalidi's colleague in the Ottoman Parliament, who had made his name opposing land sales to Jews, was working as a public inspector when he was arrested in Aleppo, Syria, sent back to Damascus, accused of harboring separatist ambitions, and hanged in May 1916. Djemal raided the offices, homes, and consuls of anyone he suspected of sedition all across the Ottoman Empire and sifted through any suspicious papers that were found. His agents searched for any additional names mentioned in these documents, and the parties in question were immediately deemed suspects and arrested.

A climate of fear hung over Jerusalem. Although formal peace talks between the Arabs and the Jews had been called off, the conviction that Djemal was willing to execute anyone who displeased him in any way led some Muslims, Jews, and Christians in Jerusalem to try to form a practical alliance and work together. In 1915, the Red Crescent Committee was created. Husayn al-Husseini, whose family was old friends with Albert Antebi, was named president; Antebi was also among the members. Wasif Jawhariyyeh worked as an assistant clerk on the committee, which held fund-raisers to collect money and clothing for the Ottoman army. The gesture was a way of demonstrating their loyalty. Few residents of Jerusalem were particularly eager to see Ottoman rule continue over the city, but by providing vital necessities to its soldiers, many hoped they could at least forestall any threats of exile or execution.

The existence of the committee also gave its members access to the Ottoman officers and officials who had taken up residence in Jerusalem. They attended their parties and solicited aid, and also forged important contacts that, in a time of war, could make a crucial difference in the ability to obtain some extra food or some other necessary good. Wasif Jawhariyyeh, whose reputation as a musician had spread throughout Jerusalem, brought his oud and a mandolin, and on the roof of whichever building was the site of that night's party, he played under the moonlight, and sang all night long, as the guests drank arak and ate fried kubeh, or little meatballs, along with other food. But even though the tensions between the Arabs and Jews had been tamped down because of the current political situation, they still ran like a current between the two groups. It was rumored, for example, that a "Miss Tanenbaum," whom Wasif Jawhariyyeh called "one of the most beautiful ladies in Jerusalem," had become Djemal's mistress after meeting him at one of the all-night parties. Through her, the Arabs insinuated, the Jews had a protector in Jerusalem in the form of Djemal.

Even if the rumors were true, they did little to improve the Jews' lot. When Djemal's military campaign in the Suez region of Egypt failed, he blamed the defeat on both the Arabs and the Jews in Jerusalem, complaining that he had been outgunned and outmanned by the British because he had been forced to keep so many troops behind in Jerusalem in order to make sure that the Arabs and Jews did not kill one another, or even worse, band together and take the city over from the Ottomans.

By the spring of 1917, British troops had marched from Egypt and were headed toward Palestine. Everyone knew that it was only a matter of time before Jerusalem fell to them. Wasif Jawhariyyeh, like most of the men his age in Jerusalem during this period, had been conscripted into the army. Sensing the end was near, he did his best to stay as far away as possible from the front lines, which had become a veritable death sentence. He had been in hiding in Jerusalem for months, sleeping at the home of a different friend every night. He had an official permit granting him leave until near the end of October 1917, and by making some changes to the dates on the document, he bought himself a few more days. But October passed, and still the British had not made their way to Jerusalem.

However bleak the conditions, people still crowded into the coffee shops, but instead of gossip they exchanged information about the progress of the army. They spoke quietly, and didn't stay out as long as they had been accustomed to, nursing a drink or playing another round of cards. The talk was hushed, in case spies were listening, and mainly it consisted of rumors and speculation, as there was very little accurate information or timely news available. With the post offices closed, the telegraphs monitored, and all forms of communication confined to the use of military officials, Jerusalem was effectively cut off from the world.

Real news was in short supply, so the people of Jerusalem did what they had always done in times of trouble: they set about trying to interpret the behavior of the person in charge. But Djemal was particularly difficult to read—mercurial, prone to bouts of rage and melancholy. He liked the trappings of the good life, smoking a cigar at the end of the day, sipping champagne at any hour, playing long games of poker that could last past midnight, taking his favorite horse out for a long ride through the Judaean wilds, racing until they both returned exhausted. He ran a city that lived in fear of him, with his sudden mood swings and arbitrary decisions that might result in yet another new body hanging from the city gates.

A naval blockade of the Mediterranean enforced by the British and their allies further exacerbated the mounting shortages. The value of Ottoman currency dropped so precipitously that even when merchants managed to get food supplies, they refused to accept the worthless money. Consumers were forced back into a system of barter, trading whatever they had left at home or whatever skills they possessed for sustenance.

At one point in 1917 Turkey blew up Jerusalem's train station, where Herzl and his friends had arrived during his 1898 visit. The station's construction had once been such a point of pride that consuls and officials came from all over the Ottoman Empire to celebrate its opening. But now the Ottomans feared that they were about to lose control of the city. Jaffa and other locations along the coast had been forcibly evacuated by Djemal, and the residents of Jerusalem feared that they would be next because of their city's strategic and symbolic importance. People started gathering whatever meager supplies they could in case they should be forced to leave at a moment's notice.

Wasif Jawhariyyeh soon learned from a friend of a new edict from the military leaders in Jericho: anyone who had not returned to Jericho immediately after a leave would be considered a traitor and hanged if caught. Jawhariyyeh still vacillated, not knowing whether to leave his hiding place in Jerusalem and take his chances back in Jericho. But, uncertain of how much longer it would take for the British to arrive in Jerusalem, he finally decided to return to his camp. Too many people recognized him in the city; it was getting harder to go out on the streets, even at night.

In December 1917, while walking in Jerusalem with his brother, he made arrangements to leave. He met with a villager and paid a small amount of money to rent a donkey to use the next morning for the trip. The brothers then went to the Armenian quarter of the Old City, where across from the Citadel near the Jaffa Gate was a storekeeper who sold weapons. Jawhariyyeh wanted to make sure that if he went back he at least had bullets for his revolver; the army was now in such dire straits that many soldiers were armed with unloaded guns.

The streets were eerie as they made their way through the once bustling Old City. Most of the shops were closed. Djemal had issued a new order that anyone discovered out walking could be arrested, so the Jawhariyyehs did their errands in a great hurry. Wasif bought some presents to give his commander in Jericho, to try to influence the way the commander might view his desertion and sudden re-emergence in the ranks.

Then, on their route, they bumped into someone whom Jawhariyyeh recognized, one of the Ottoman commanders who was in charge of arresting suspected army deserters. He was accompanied by a small group of soldiers, who would surround any young man of army age they encountered on their patrols and demand his papers to see if they were in order. If they were not, the man was arrested on the spot—a fate Jawhariyyeh was certain would be his. He braced himself for the inevitable, but when his acquaintance spotted him, for a brief moment there was a flash of old times in Jerusalem.

The officer, recognizing the young musician from the many evenings he had played the oud, sung Arabic songs, and drunk arak on one Jerusalem rooftop or another, saluted him with a "How are you, my son?" and walked on, not bothering to demand the papers he surely knew that Jawhariyyeh did not possess.

That incident occurred on one of the last nights of Turkish control of Jerusalem. Despite his preparations, Jawhariyyeh never went back to the army. The Turkish and German armies had already started to depart from Jerusalem and withdraw to Constantinople, leaving the city a shambles. "Turkish soldiers were looting whatever fell into their hands," Jawhariyyeh later wrote in a journal he kept of this time. "Some of them attacked the houses in a horrendous way. The people were offering them food to get rid of their evil presence. We fed several Turkish soldiers. The sound of artillery hitting Jerusalem and its villages became louder." Everywhere in Jerusalem, the sounds of war could be heard as the British army moved inexorably toward the city. The people braced yet again for change.

3

By 1915, Khalil Sakakini was uncertain how much longer he would be allowed to remain in Jerusalem. When he spoke with friends who had contacts in Djemal's office, he was told that it looked as if "they were preparing to banish me from Jerusalem," he wrote in his journal in March that year.

In trying to determine what he had done wrong, he had arrived at two possibilities: First, as a Christian, he was assumed by the Ottomans to favor a Russian, French, and English victory in the war. Second, he worried that they disapproved of the fact that he had founded a school in the city that educated its students in what he called a "national spirit," encouraging them not to think of themselves as Christians, Muslims, or Jews but as Arabs, part of a wider Arabic culture.

Two forces had become even more intense in Jerusalem in the wake of the war's outbreak—religion and nationalism. The tenuous thread of coexistence between the different religious and ethnic groups in Jerusalem was starting to unravel. In the mosques, the imams who stood up and spoke at the end of services were calling the war a "jihad," a holy war. The government's rhetoric also began to reflect a perception that this was a war in which Muslims fought the Christian world.

In this kind of atmosphere, even people who were disinclined to do so were forced to choose sides. The boundaries between the different groups in the city that had once been easily crossed at parties, in coffee shops, or in all-night poker games now seemed drawn that much more sharply.

Sakakini was determined to remain in Jerusalem. Having turned thirty-eight that year, he spent the months after his birthday going from office to office, trying to press his case that staying in the city and keeping his school afloat constituted a way of doing army service far more fruitfully then being sent to the front or to a remote town. But even as he navigated his way through the Ottoman bureaucracy, he realized that a new, more uncertain time had begun in Jerusalem. In his journal in 1915, he had struggled to define himself in the new Jerusalem. "I am not a Christian and not a Buddhist, not a Muslim and not a Jew. . . . I am just one from the human race," he had written. But it was a struggle even for him to maintain this illusion.

One day in December 1917, with the British advancing ever closer to the city gates, a knock came at the Sakakini door in the Old City. There stood Alter Levine, a Jew, announcing that the Ottomans were trying to arrest him, and asking that Sakakini hide him.

In Sakakini's moment of decision, so many of the issues confronting Jerusalem at that time were played out. He hesitated at first, fearing, rightfully, that taking in a man wanted for questioning would only bring danger to himself and his family, and in the days of Djemal's rule, people had been hanged for less serious crimes. And yet if Saka-kini believed in the principles of hospitality required by the Arabic culture, the principles he promoted in his own school, and even more so, if he believed in the fundamental message of Jerusalem—that some deeper sense of fellowship bound the disparate communities of the city together, that there was a value to being able to declare oneself a resident of the city of Jerusalem—then how could he not take Levine in, despite the personal risk to himself? "The man sought refuge with me and I could do nothing other than welcome him in," Sakakini wrote. "I said to myself that he is not really seek-ing refuge with me per se, but rather with my people, as represented in my individual personality. He is seeking refuge in the social graces of my cultural idiom . . ."

The pull of the old Jerusalem won, and Sakakini hid Levine in his house. But Levine ended up inadvertently drawing the police to the house one day by sending word to his mother-in-law that he wanted her to send food; he refused to eat what Sakakini offered him because it was not kosher. One of the many spies on the street must have noticed her coming and going, because one day, Levine's mother-in-law in tow, a knock came at the front door, and both men were ar-rested. On the last day of Turkish rule in Jerusalem, December 10, 1917, the two men, tied together with the same rope, were sent to a Damascus jail.

Sakakini was released a year later and waited for permission to return to Jerusalem, which was now under the control of the British. During that period he became more deeply involved in the bur-geoning Arab nationalist movement in the region. But even as he sat in the Damascus coffee shops and declared to friends that he was "first of all, an Arab," he continued to visit Levine in jail until Levine's own release three months later. Amid the war and revolts and the triumph of nationalism, there were still some who put the personal above the political.

4

All through the war years, people made peace with their parting from the Jerusalem they had once known. Many had been forced to leave the city, being either called up for military service, deported, or exiled. Many of those who survived the war eventually returned, but by then Jerusalem was under the control of new conquerors, and yet another layer took shape upon the remains of the city's past.

Years later, after the state of Israel had been founded and the Israeli-Palestinian conflict was well under way, many looked back, trying to pinpoint the moment when they realized that that conflict was inevitable. David Ben-Gurion, who became Israel's first prime minister, said it was the day in 1915 that he sat on a train waiting to leave Jerusalem at the order of Djemal, who banished many known Zionist activists from the city.

Ben-Gurion had tried to turn himself into an Ottoman—studying Turkish, attending law school in Constantinople, trying to organize a Jewish legion to fight on behalf of the Ottoman Empire in the war, and even donning a red fez. But all these gestures had been to no avail, for at the end of the day, Djemal had looked at him and seen not an Ottoman but an advocate for a future Jewish state, and had him jailed in Jerusalem.

Ben-Gurion later wrote that no one in the Jewish community was brave enough to come visit him other than Albert Antebi. Upon his release from jail, he was exiled to Alexandria. Later, in his books and memoirs, he recalled vividly a particular moment on the train, when an Arab acquaintance of his, whom he called Yeya Effendi, walked by and saw him waiting to leave. The men embraced, exchanged news and greetings, and then Yeya Effendi asked him where he was going.

Ben-Gurion told him that he was being exiled, ordered never to return to Jerusalem. Yeya Effendi held him in the embrace of a true friend, mourning his loss of their shared city. Then he looked at Ben-Gurion and said something that Ben-Gurion pondered for the entire train ride to Alexandria. "As your friend, I am sad," Yeya Effendi told him. "But as an Arab, I rejoice."

5

For Wasif Jawhariyyeh, the turning point was likely an incident that took place after Jerusalem was already in the hands of the British.

Despite being Orthodox Christian, Jawhariyyeh's father had insisted to his son that, as an Arab, in order that he might truly speak and love Arabic as a language, and understand and be part of Arab culture, it was his duty to study and appreciate the Koran. Girgis Jawhariyyeh had trained as a lawyer and so was familiar with Muslim religious law. As a youngster growing up in Jerusalem, Wasif memorized Islam's holy book alongside Muslim boys.

There was a well-known story about Wasif's father that circulated around Jerusalem, and that Wasif himself recorded in his diary. One day, as the elder Jawhariyyeh was taking his regular walk around their Jerusalem neighborhood with one of his closest friends, they passed near the Jaffa Gate, where Wasif's father encountered several Muslim acquaintances, all respected figures in the city.

The men were greeting one another politely, exchanging pleasant-
ries, when a dog happened to walk by them. "Ya Abu Khalil," one of
the Muslim men said, referring to Wasif's father by his honorific title,
the name of his eldest son, "would you say this dog is a Muslim or a
Christian?"

This was a provocative question, because Muslims do not consider dogs to be clean animals, and to call a man a dog is to gravely
insult him. But Wasif's father deflected the potentially explosive
situation with a witty response. "It should be easy to find out, my
dear sir," he replied. "Today, Friday, is our fasting day. You can throw
him a bone. If he picks it up, he is definitely not a Christian."

By the war's end it was almost impossible to imagine a joke like
that being told without a fight ensuing, so small had the amount of
common space shared by the different religious and ethnic groups
in Jerusalem become.

In his journal, Wasif Jawhariyyeh recorded that on a Sunday
morning in April, probably around 1919 or 1920, he went with a
group of Muslim friends to a bar in the Old City to have a drink. It
was a warm, sunny day, and the friends wanted to enjoy Jerusalem.
They bought sacks of green almonds from one of the vendors in the
market and decided to walk together to the Dome of the Rock to sit
outside in its courtyard, have a picnic, and watch the flow of people,
the colors and sounds that made the city such a special place. But
when they arrived at the compound, they saw troops posted outside
each of the main gates.

The soldiers on duty that day were part of a Muslim Indian army
contingent employed by the British to help patrol Jerusalem. The
British did not want anyone who was not Muslim to enter the area
where the mosque was located, as there was growing ethnic conflict
in the city, and they feared a problem erupting at a holy site. As
people waited in long lines to enter, the guards would ask, "Musli-

man?" If the response was "no," they were sent away. When Jawhari-yyeh's turn came and the soldier asked if he was a Muslim, he answered, "Thank God, Musliman," even though he was not. Behind him, one of his friends shouted out, vouching for him, "I swear to God, Musliman." He later recorded in his journal, "Imagine, dear reader, the idea of Wasif ben Girgis Jawhariyyeh being a Muslim," clearly relishing such a moment when he was able to blur the lines of community and identity.

Jawhariyyeh was waved through the gates, but when one of his Muslim friends reached the head of the line, he decided to have some fun at his expense and told the Indian guard, "This [man] is a Jew, not a Muslim." And since the friend, known in the journal as al-Zardaq, had fair coloring, the Indian guard believed Jawhariyyeh and raised his gun in al-Zardaq's face, barring him from taking another step forward.

All of Jawhariyyeh's friends started to laugh, even as al-Zardaq grew red in the face from anger and started yelling, "What, my name is Muhammad and I'm prevented from entering the Haram [the Noble Sanctuary compound where the mosque is located], while you, Wasif, are treated like a graduate of al-Azhar [a famous Muslim center of learning in Egypt] and a pious Muslim?"

As al-Zardaq ran to another gate—only to be stopped by another guard who was alerted to his presence by the soldier blowing his whistle—Jawhariyyeh recalled, "We threw ourselves on the green grass in the court of the Haram, eating green almonds with al-Zardaq outside thundering against Wasif." He did not realize then that guards asking people to declare to which religious group they belonged had become a permanent part of the landscape. The days of friends of different religions sharing picnics on the rolling green meadow outside the Dome of the Rock were over.

6

Neither Ruhi Khalidi nor Albert Antebi—rivals, collaborators, devotees of Jerusalem—survived to see the changes wrought by the war.

Khalidi had passed away suddenly in 1913, in Constantinople, where he was working on his book about Zionism and preparing for the next session of Parliament. That book recorded his shifting political views. Toward its end, he expressed anger that the Ottoman government had not taken a stronger and more aggressive stance against what he saw as Zionist efforts to gain control over Palestine. Still, it was impossible to know for certain if he would have fully embraced Arab nationalism had he survived the war. He apparently took ill with typhoid and succumbed after only a few days. His older brother, Thurayya, came from Jerusalem to collect his belongings, among them his unfinished manuscript, which the family never published.

Later, after the British were firmly ensconced in Jerusalem and had issued in 1917 the Balfour Declaration, which lent their government's official support to the idea of a Jewish homeland in Palestine— an act that Jawhariyyeh called in his own journal "the loss of our homeland"—relatives of Khalidi suggested that he had actually been poisoned for his Arab nationalist ideas and his advocacy against Zionism.

During the war Albert Antebi was also at work on a document describing his vision for the future, and it was clear that in it he no longer saw his place as being in Palestine. In 1914, soon after the war broke out, he had complained that the Zionists "claimed to be the only heirs of tomorrow." He recognized that this left him and others who shared his worldview as part of the past. The Zionists, he noted, had "conquered Palestine from the Arabs, Turkey, the European powers and the non-Zionist Jews." In papers found in his briefcase after he died, he argued that the region should be divided into cantons, with different groups controlling each one and the entire country overseen by France.

Antebi did not leave Jerusalem willingly. As he had always done, he managed to ingratiate himself with the new power in the city when the war broke out, and became Djemal's confidant and assistant. But although Antebi might not consider himself a Zionist, he was involved in activities that Djemal, who was suspicious of virtually everyone around him, deemed threatening to the cohesion of the Ottoman Empire.

By October 1916, Antebi's fortunes had changed. Invited to dine one evening at Djemal's headquarters in Jerusalem, he and his wife walked home later that night talking about the fine evening they had just enjoyed. The very next day, a knock came at the door shortly after breakfast, and soldiers entered and announced that the family was being sent into exile in Damascus. The Antebis barely had time to pack a few belongings and leave. Such were the vagaries of fortune in Jerusalem during wartime.

As an Ottoman citizen, Antebi was drafted into service as a foot soldier and sent to fight at the front. When the armistice was signed in November 1918, he made his way back to Constantinople, hungry, sick, and tired. His older children had been scattered throughout Europe when the war broke out, but his wife and younger children reunited with him in Constantinople. The embassy of France had reopened its doors there as soon as the war ended, and Antebi, his connections still intact, was hired to help repatriate refugees streaming into the city, eager to return to their homes and rebuild their lives.

In December 1918, Antebi wrote to his friends that their situation was difficult. "We have been severed from all news since August. . . . We are embarrassed with our lack of money, there is a growing famine. . . . We have no break from the flu. . . . Is it over? We fear not." When he reflected on why he had been forced to leave Jerusalem, he concluded that he had been exiled for the crime "of having doubled the size of the Jewish land in Palestine." As much as he loved Jerusalem, he believed that he no longer had a place in the city.

In January 1919, he was still working at the French embassy and had just helped fourteen hundred people board ships bound for Syria and Palestine. The work was satisfying but he decided the time had come to finally go back to France and rebuild his life in Marseille. "Your mother needs rest," he wrote to his eldest children, who all returned safely to France and were awaiting their parents' return. "Her health is wobbly since the typhoid fever and the great privations have weakened everyone. . . . We will come home to France and most likely stay there."

This was his last letter home. In February 1919, Antebi was admitted to the emergency room of a French hospital in Constantinople, ill from fever, the victim of another epidemic sweeping the city. In March 1919, at the age of forty-five, he died.

Antebi's family recounted many stories about him, but there was one that was especially moving, and seemed a fitting end to his experiences of wartime Jerusalem. At around the time that the British conquered Jerusalem—probably in 1918, near the end of the conflict— Antebi was still in the army with his unit in Damascus. He was standing in line at an outdoor market with other soldiers trying to get food when suddenly he spied Djemal. Barefoot, thin and weak from lack of food and care, his clothes in tatters after years in the army, Antebi called out to the former governor of Jerusalem, who was now making his way through the town surrounded by soldiers.

Djemal's guards made a move to stop Antebi from approaching, but Djemal recognized him and held them off. One can imagine the scene even now—the beggar from Jerusalem confronting the man who he felt symbolized the forces that had destroyed his city.

He called out to Djemal, his voice urgent and pressing. He had an important question to ask, one that echoes down to our own time. In anguish, Antebi cried out, "What have you done to my Jerusalem?"

Ruhi Khalidi and Albert Antebi had always shared a central conviction: despite the conflicts of recent years, they ultimately saw themselves, and each other, as Ottomans. Their protests, their fights, their struggles for power were all carried out under the corrupt but protective and sustaining embrace of the four-hundred-year-old Ottoman rule in Jerusalem. They understood the contradictions in their own identities, but they believed sincerely that one could be simultaneously a loyal Ottoman and pledged to a national, ethnic, or religious cause. In the end, they were proven wrong.

7

The British found themselves in possession of a battle-scarred city, its streets gray and dreary, its people debilitated from the privations of war. Jerusalem was once again a capital, though, and the British set out to remake the city in their own image, just as previous conquerors had done. One of the first things they did was to build a broad avenue through the center of what was being called the "New City," the area built outside the walls of the Old City, and named it after King George V. They planned the thoroughfare as the linchpin of a revitalized city, and as the years went by, the idea started to take on a life of its own. At the end of the street, they constructed a beautiful and imposing luxury hotel, the King David, with an open veranda where waiters in crisp white uniforms served tea and pastries. With time it became the place to be seen in Jerusalem, and even the mayor got his hair cut there, greeting people with a nod or a wave as they passed. In 1946 a Jewish militant group opposed to the British presence in Palestine, led by the future prime minister of Israel, Menachem Begin, set off a bomb there.

Across the street from the King David Hotel rose the towering YMCA building, with its stained-glass windows portraying the twelve tribes of Israel, designed by the same architectural team that built the Empire State Building in New York City. Its spire gave a commanding view of the city, and later, during the war that broke out between the Arabs and the Israelis after the state of Israel was founded, snipers took aim from its windows to shoot at people in the streets.

The British governor of Jerusalem, Ronald Storrs, was an ardent Christian, who was now responsible for running the city that had dominated his childhood imagination. He tore down the Ottoman clock tower that the city's residents had once set their watches by, and commissioned new street signs to be made by Armenian potters from the Old City, who were famous for their rich colors and designs evoking biblical motifs. He issued a number of edicts intended to control the city's future design. No one was allowed to build with any material other than stone—a tradition that is maintained in Jerusalem to this day—and soon the entire city took on the same creamy hue, glowing in the afternoons with a golden cast.

Khalil Sakakini, who had made his way back to Jerusalem from jail in Damascus, noted that the city's residents had already started to accommodate themselves to the British in the same way that the buildings' façades had. They began drinking tea rather than black coffee, they offered guests cigarettes rather than a water pipe, they sent their children to schools to learn English. "Only I remain a nationalist," lamented Sakakini.

Jerusalem became a city of men wearing pith helmets and women walking the streets at midday toting parasols. The British hosted formal parties, and the ladies ate sticky Arab sweets like baklava without removing their long white gloves, delicately licking the honey off the fingertips. They organized fox and jackal hunts in the swamps north of the city and formed social clubs, usually based on familial or social ties from the schools they had attended back home. Soon there was an active and regular season of musicals, plays, and performances.

The British families liked to picnic on the sites of ancient biblical cities, spreading out blankets and climbing amid the ruins. Sometimes they went skiing in Lebanon, or organized long horseback rides into the valleys. At night, a poker game at the governor's house could last well into the next day. The governor had built a ballroom with chandeliers where dances were held regularly, and couples twirled to the latest tunes under the stern visages of the imposing portraits of British royalty that hung on the walls. In the yard of the governor's house was a cemetery for their pet dogs, many killed during the regular hunting expeditions they sponsored. They hosted frequent athletic competitions and relished the sight of races and tennis games set against the backdrop of Jerusalem's ancient skyline.

Jerusalem seemed to expand in all directions in the years after the war, and distinct Jewish and Arab neighborhoods began to take shape. David Kroyanker, an Israeli architect who has written extensively about Jerusalem's architectural history, noted that in the Jewish neighborhoods that sprang up, "the conquest of Jerusalem by the Zionist ethos" could be seen. The Zionists had debated whether to try to form a block of settlements close together or in disparate places around the city. In the end, they had opted for contiguous blocks, and soon a wall of Jewish neighborhoods, "in the shape of a half-crescent moon," Kroyanker noted, emerged around the Old City.

Under British rule an estimated fifty new neighborhoods were constructed in Jerusalem, and probably two-thirds of them were Jewish. They were built with an eye to providing communal services, small mini-states in the making, each one with its own health clinic, synagogue, and public schools, set along roads that led into the city center. The neighborhoods had large public gardens. Arab construction during this period was still organized more along private lines, the homes built and funded by family members who wanted to live together, with few public buildings or communal services. The Arabs still needed to travel into the British-run city for their health care and other municipal services.

Arthur Ruppin had spent most of the war in Constantinople, living in the Pera Palace, a hotel that, like most of the city's residents at that time, was down on its luck but still clung to its previous respectability. He liked to go to the club next door, nurse a cup of coffee, and peruse as many newspapers as possible to try to get a handle on what was happening in Palestine and around the world. He had always been a careful consumer of news, a strategist, able to read between the lines of any given story. He realized that the days of Turkish rule in Jerusalem were coming to a close. By 1918, he was back in Jerusalem, and the reversal of his and Djemal's fortunes did not go unnoted in his diary: "When [Djemal] told me two years ago that I would NEVER return to Palestine, could he have imagined that he would now be fleeing from Turkey, cursed and hated by all, and that the Jews would have been assured of Palestine under the protection of the Allies?"

The Balfour Declaration had been issued only the previous year. The document was actually a three-sentence letter stating that the British government had agreed to support the establishment of a

Jewish national home in Palestine. The letter had grown out of the sympathies of several British cabinet ministers with the Zionist movement, and the warm relationship they maintained with the indefatigable Chaim Weizmann, who had done some scientific research that contributed to the British war effort and who throughout the war continued to speak with government leaders about Zionism. This was what Herzl had been seeking back in Jerusalem in 1898: formal recognition of the Jewish connection to Palestine by a power that controlled the country. Ruppin had already drawn up a thirty-year settlement plan while he was still drinking coffee in Constantinople. "The work will not be easy," he acknowledged. "Whatever the future may hold, this much is certain: in our wildest dreams, we did not imagine the Great War would leave us so much."

The British had made promises not only to the Jews regarding Palestine. Letters had also been exchanged in 1915–16 during the war when the British were trying to gain Arab support in their battle against the Ottoman Empire; the Arabs had understood these overtures to mean that Palestine, among other areas, would be theirs after the Ottomans were routed. At first the British were so preoccupied with their administration of Jerusalem that they did not realize that the tensions between the Jewish and Arab communities were growing steadily worse. It soon became clear, however, that any notion that this tension could somehow be resolved by trying to create an inclusive Palestinian identity—one that both Arabs and Jews could adopt, share, and shape together—was a futile proposition.

In 1919, with the war barely over and negotiations on the future of Europe still under way, the first Palestinian Arab Congress met in Haifa to try to coordinate a strategy to cope with a new influx of Jewish immigrants who had begun arriving in greater and greater numbers. Soon riots broke out in Jerusalem during religious festivals, and in 1929 violence in Hebron left members of the ancient

Jewish community that had lived there for centuries dead at the hands of their neighbors. Hundreds more on both sides were killed or wounded before the British regained control of the city.

By the beginning of the 1930s, it was impossible to miss the signs of growing nationalism on both sides. Clubs promoted, respectively, Arabic and Arab culture, or Hebrew and Jewish culture. Acts of terrorism became more widespread and more violent. Jerusalem bore the brunt of the mounting tensions, for unlike Tel Aviv, which had consciously been built by the Zionists as a separate city, growing up alongside its Arab-dominated neighbor Jaffa, Jerusalem was still shared by Arabs and Jews alike. The city's history and religious significance effectively mapped out a maze of interconnecting, overlapping neighborhoods.

In 1934 Arthur Ruppin listed in his journal the many recent successes that he had seen the Zionists accrue: fifty thousand Jewish immigrants had arrived, the Huleh Valley (where the British governor had loved hunting foxes) had been acquired for settlement, and a Zionist communal identity was becoming more evident. It was a successful year, he concluded, but this very success, he knew, would give rise to another set of problems: "I am convinced that the Arabs will not be content to watch our progress passively and that we will one day experience serious disturbances in the country." In January 1935, during a talk with Chaim Weizmann, who would become the first president of the future state of Israel, Ruppin had told him, "For the next few years, we are in my opinion in a latent state of war; if we do not make use of this period to become numerically stronger, we are lost."

Ruppin's political instincts had always been acute. On the Arab side he detected a feeling that the tide was somehow turning in favor of the Jews. In 1935, when Khalil Sakakini traveled around Palestine as part of his job as a school inspector, he still saw mainly what he called "Arab land," swaths of Arab villages where life was still lived in a traditional way, the outsides of the homes decorated with horseshoes for good luck or hamsas in the shape of a hand, with a blue stone in the center to ward off the evil eye. But Sakakini knew that the Jews were continuing to buy land, and that each day ships were arriving at the Jaffa port filled with Jewish refugees, especially now that tensions in Europe were mounting with the rise of the Nazis to power. At a party one of Sakakini's friends had suggested only half-jokingly that if the Arabs wanted to maintain a future in Palestine, they would do well to learn Hebrew. Sakakini had been affronted by the remark, which he perceived as a sign of weakness, of despair, and of a growing sense of Arab helplessness in the face of a Jewish settlement movement that could not be countered or stopped.

The gains the Jews were making might not yet have been evident when Sakakini traveled outside Jerusalem, but he tried to imagine a situation where "the Arabs will continue to sell land and the Jews will continue to buy it." When he speculated about the consequences, he knew the map of Palestine would be permanently transformed and predicted, "and then there will be no choice but to wake up . . . no choice but to act."

Sakakini did not then propose any specific actions he thought the Arabs might take, but in fact by now, both sides were rapidly arming themselves. Still, no one uttered the word "war" in Jerusalem. With the British firmly ensconced, the city had outwardly taken on the air of a British colony, genteel and formally polite. But just below the surface, Jerusalem seethed. There was a palpable undercurrent of tension, and even small, seemingly insignificant matters could cause a stir. The British had decided to establish a national radio station, called Radio Palestine, and began broadcasting in both Hebrew and Arabic. But Arabs were outraged when, during the Hebrew broadcasts, the word "Palestine" was translated into Hebrew as "Eretz

Yisrael," or the Land of Israel, a biblical term that signaled to listeners that Palestine itself was only a temporary geographic aberration, and the place would always be the Land of Israel, promised to the Jews by God in the Bible.

Sakakini, so sensitive to the nuances of language, had called to complain. "If Palestine is the Land of Israel, then we the Arabs are foreign citizens," he thundered to the head of the station, declaring that he intended to boycott it from then on. Eventually, the British warned the Jews to stop referring to Palestine by anything other than its proper name on the air, but the warning made little difference.

That type of dispute soon came to seem minor, however, in the wake of the violence that shook Jerusalem and eventually all of Palestine. In April 1939, six Arab leaders had met and formed what became known as the Arab High Command, led by Haj Amin al-Husseini, the scion of the prominent Jerusalem family that had once been such close friends with Albert Antebi. As a response to what they saw as British support of Zionism, the High Command called for a strike of Arab workers and a boycott of Jewish products. Jewish settlements were soon attacked by roving Arab guerrilla forces, as were British soldiers. Bridges were blown up, convoys came under fire, phone lines were cut, and mail vans were stolen. In Jaffa, Jewish-owned orchards were burned to the ground. A group of Jews coming out of the popular Edison movie theater in downtown Jerusalem were shot and killed. Now that the violence that Sakakini had foretold had broken out, he worried about where it might lead: "I pray to God the end will be good."

Arthur Ruppin found himself frequently involved in disagreements over how the Jews should respond. Some wanted to revive the peace talks that had been initiated in 1913 and then suspended because of the war. Ruppin himself even joined a new group called Brit Shalom, which advocated attempting to find a way for the two sides to share Palestine. But he began to find himself increasingly at odds with his friends, who continued to adhere to the idea that Herzl himself had promoted: namely, that eventually the Arabs would realize the economic advantages the Zionist movement brought to Palestine and come to terms with their presence in the country. Ruppin now found himself taking the position that rational approaches such as these had no relevance for the tribal conflict that existed between the Jews and the Arabs. Political conflicts were not governed by "rational arguments," he told them, "but by instincts."

The Zionists could argue until they were breathless about the benefits of their economic and social plans, but this would not "move the Arabs to relinquish what they believe to be their power over Palestine to the Jews or to share it with the Jews, as long as they are the overwhelming majority here," Ruppin wrote. The Zionists would achieve nothing by asking the Arabs for concessions, or making concessions to the Arabs, for that matter. Rather, they had to create a situation in which accepting the Jewish presence in Palestine was not a choice but rather "a question of coming to terms with reality."

When Ruppin spoke privately he referred to the coming conflict as "the decisive struggle." In March 1938, he wrote about a typical incident of that period in Jerusalem. At 7 p.m. one night, a bomb had been thrown at Jews strolling down Jaffa Road, one of the key thoroughfares in the city, where a lively commerce of shops and cafés had sprung up. Three people had been seriously hurt and ten more suffered minor injuries, Ruppin recorded. Then an hour later, two bombs were thrown at two nearby Arab coffee shops, killing one customer and injuring twenty to thirty others. No one had taken responsibility for either action, but it was viewed by the residents as another skirmish between the Arabs and the Jews.

The British response was to impose a curfew for the following day. Everyone was ordered to be in his home by 7 p.m. When Ruppin reflected on the incident, he saw it as the harbinger of things to come—"terrible mutual murder," he predicted. Maybe now people would realize that "the Jews are and will remain in Palestine, and that they cannot be disposed of by acts of terrorism, which will only lead to terrorism from our side."

Ruppin tried to devise a plan that might achieve his goal of buying time and peace in which the Zionists could achieve their goals of purchasing more land and settling more immigrants. Even if there was eventually some entity designated as a Jewish state in Palestine, he argued, it was essentially meaningless unless there was a Jewish majority living within its borders. Ruppin did not want to replace the British just yet, but instead put forth an idea of Jewish autonomy within the mechanism of municipal associations—not unlike the idea of Jewish and Arab cantons in Palestine that had been found scrawled in Albert Antebi's papers after his death. This would enable the Jews to run their own lives as much as possible in areas of Palestine where the inhabitants were predominantly or solely Jewish. "In this way, I avoid internal friction with Arabs," Ruppin explained. Eventually, he saw these municipal associations expanding and combining into a much larger Jewish commonwealth, or even a state. But for now, the guiding principle was that Jews would be able to constitute a majority in at least some sections of Palestine.

The political situation continued to deteriorate, though, and Ruppin's proposal never had a chance to be tested. The British eventually sent a commission to Palestine to investigate and find ways to stop what was being called the Great Arab Revolt. In a report issued in 1937, the commission concluded that the Arab and Zionist positions regarding Palestine's future were "irreconcilable." The British themselves were at a loss about how to solve the problem, and at first suggested a partition, dividing Palestine into Arab and Jewish states, with the British themselves keeping control over Jerusalem, as well as Nazareth and Bethlehem, two cities strongly associated with the history of Christianity. The Jews rejected the proposed British boundaries, although they accepted the concept of a partition in Palestine; the Arabs, for their part, refused to consider partition. Even the British eventually decided that the idea was impractical and probably impossible to implement. When the fighting broke out again a few months after the commission's visit, the British put it down with brutal force, and deported many of the Arab leaders. The Hagannah, the underground militia that had grown out of the forces the Jews set up prior to the war to protect the settlements, was now allowed to organize officially. They were deployed not only to guard Jewish settlements against Arab attacks but also to launch their own reprisal missions.

By 1942, Khalil Sakakini was writing in his diary that he saw one of only two possible ways to end the fighting: either the Arabs would remain in control of the land, or the Jews would undertake to assume that control. War was inevitable.

Later that year, in a scene that harked back to an earlier era in Jerusalem, Sakakini found himself at a café with a large group of men. All afternoon long, they drank and smoked. People came and sat for a while and then left, their seats taken by others who happened to walk by. The discussion, as it always did, quickly turned to politics. What would be the future of Palestine? Who would control it? How would the mounting conflict between the Jews and the Arabs end?

Sakakini found himself debating with one of the men. They had never met, but they continued to spar back and forth. After a while, someone thought to formally introduce them. "This is Khalil Sakakini, the famous Arab educator," the man said, "and this is Judah Magnes, the president and founder of the Hebrew University." Magnes was a member of the same political group as Arthur Ruppin, Brit Shalom. It must have been a strange moment for Sakakini when he realized with whom he had been arguing. When Ruppin's dream of founding a Hebrew national university in Jerusalem on Mount Scopus had come true, and British officials gathered with him and Magnes in 1921 to lay the cornerstone for the new institution, Sakakini had stood outside the Dome of the Rock mosque and given a speech opposing the university. His fiery oratory had helped establish his reputation in the city as a leading Arab nationalist.

Sakakini did not mention the incident, and Magnes was gracious and effusive after learning his identity. He told Sakakini that he had learned Arabic by studying and practicing from the Arabic textbooks that Sakakini had written. Sakakini tried to find a way to explain to Magnes how he viewed the current political situation in Palestine, and why he vehemently disagreed with Magnes's proposition that the two sides could share the country. Typically, he illustrated his point with a story.

One day, he said, a man was riding on a donkey to a city. It might even have been a city very much like Jerusalem.

On the way, he met another man walking in the road.

It was a hot day, and the man in the road looked tired after such a long journey. "Why do you walk?" the donkey's owner asked. "Come, let us ride together on the donkey."

The grateful traveler climbed onto the donkey, and the two men rode together in peace. A short while later, the traveler leaned over and observed to the owner, "How fast your donkey is."

They rode on, getting closer to their destination. At this point, they might have reached the section of the road to Jerusalem where the hills grow steep, and the air starts to shimmer, and the contours of the city can be seen rising in the mist in the distance. Viewing this beautiful sight, a man could get lost. "How fast our donkey is," the man now told the donkey's owner.

The owner of the donkey brought his animal to a stop. He turned to his traveling companion and ordered, "Get off the donkey."

The traveler was confused. What had he done wrong? "Why?"

he asked the donkey's owner, perplexed by the sudden change in his fortunes. The donkey's owner replied, "I fear that soon you will say, 'How fast *my* donkey is.'"

Only six years later, in 1948, the state of Israel would be established. War would come once again, and once again Jerusalem would tremble, uncertain of its fate. Khalil Sakakini and his daughter would pack a small bag—just a few clothes and some personal belongings—and leave the besieged city, expecting to return after the war ended. But he would never live in Jerusalem again. Judah Magnes would die shortly after delivering a speech before the United Nations in favor of the founding of the state of Israel and be buried in Jerusalem. All this remained in the future, a destiny still unfolding. For now, at least, the two men companiably shared a table in Jerusalem.

Jerusalem 2004–2006

And they spread among the Israelites a bad report
about the land they had explored.
They said, "The land we explored devours those living in it."

—NUMBERS 13:32

1

One June morning in 2004 I made my way through the Old City of Jerusalem, headed to the Khalidi Library.

I felt a slight chill as I walked through the deserted market that led to the entrance of the library. The market had always been the most vibrant part of the city. On any day, you might hear someone declaiming about politics from a table at an outdoor café, shop owners calling out to the crowds that thronged by them, trying to get their attention, the braying of donkeys being led through the narrow, busy streets. There were always groups of tourists sightseeing and bargaining over trinkets, leather coats, decorated tiles, and the other items piled up in stores in teetering pyramids that might topple over into the street at any moment. Men clutched bags of sunflower seeds or pistachio nuts that they cracked and ate as they talked with their friends, gesticulating to make a point. The women walked arm in arm, occasionally emitting a sharp whistle or cry as their children ran too far ahead of them.

But now the market was empty, the oppressive silence the result of the constant beat of terrorism over the past few years. When I heard loud steps behind me, I jumped and turned around quickly, not knowing what to expect. It was an Israeli patrol, the only other sign of humanity on the street that day. The soldiers walked by me quickly, guns ready, scanning the area, barely acknowledging my presence. On the wall next to me graffiti in Hebrew noted that on the very spot where I now walked, a Jewish yeshiva student had been murdered as he made his way to pray at the Wailing Wall.

The Khalidi Library was in the same building as it had been back in 1913, when Ruhi Khalidi paid his final visit to it before returning to Constantinople and his untimely death from typhoid. It was situated on Bab al-Silsila, or Chain Street, one of the most trod-upon thoroughfares in the Old City because it led to the Wailing Wall, the Holy Sepulchre, and the Dome of the Rock mosque, sites holy to Jews, Christians, and Muslims. This was the dividing line between Albert Antebi's world and that of Ruhi Khalidi, the street that served as the border between the Jewish and Muslim quarters of the Old City and witnessed the uneasy peace that existed between the neighborhoods.

As I hurried toward the library, I bumped into Haifa Khalidi, its current caretaker, coming to meet me. When Sheik Mohammad Sunallah Khalidi founded the collection as part of a religious endowment, he had decreed that the books and library were intended "only for men." But now a woman was in charge, having taken over after her father died. She was slim and wore glasses, her short hair graying and neatly cut. Today she was dressed in a skirt that reached just below her knees and a brown short-sleeved sweater. She greeted me and then unlocked the door to the library.

One of the most amazing things about Jerusalem is how secretive the city is, not easily yielding its treasures to outsiders. Had Haifa Khalidi not come to meet me, I would have passed the building without even a second glance. The exterior door was nondescript, one more in a row. Only a small sign at the entrance, with the library's name written in French and Arabic and the inscription "Within are precious books" announced its presence. The plain, discreet exterior gave way to a beautiful inner sanctum, a room with wood paneling and a quiet, still air that seemed to block out all the sounds of the outside.

Back in 1913 the library had been stacked from floor to ceiling with bookcases, shelves, and cabinets, and the most valuable documents were kept in a French safe in the corner. The rules were posted on the wall: the library was open from 9 a.m. to 12 p.m., and then, after an afternoon lunch, 2 p.m. until one hour before sunset. The smoking of cigarettes and water pipes, the rules stated, was strictly forbidden, "regardless of who is concerned." Readers were also warned not to engage in "excessive conversation, shouting or argument."

The founding of the library in the early part of the century had also been intended to send a message that the rules on the wall sought to reinforce: in here, at least, all were equal. Its holdings had been assembled from all over the Ottoman Empire, linking Jerusalem with the wider world beyond, offering access to new ideas. Ruhi Khalidi's uncle, Yusuf, had contributed a collection that included the works of Plato, Voltaire, Darwin, Dante, and Shakespeare. Ruhi himself, who had been one of the driving forces in making the library more accessible to the wider public, had a special interest in French writers and intellectuals like Montesquieu and Victor Hugo.

Haifa Khalidi showed me the visitors' log, where guests were asked to sign in. Over the years, many scholars had passed through and left comments in a variety of languages, including Hebrew. But some of the older traditions were no longer maintained. In Ruhi Khalidi's time, during the month of Ramadan or on special feast days, the Khalidis had opened the courtyard of the library to the public and distributed sweets and food to the poor. The custom had lapsed during World War II when food was scarce and then, in the tumult surrounding the founding of the state of Israel, had never been revived.

Until recently the library itself had been in a general state of decline, as it wasn't easy to fix books that were damaged or broken. Heat and dust had taken their toll, and some of the manuscripts were in very fragile condition. Others had been borrowed and then never returned. Some were taken by family members who left Jerusalem for Beirut. Many of those were damaged during the years of fighting in Lebanon.

The library had also struggled financially. When the family had first considered trying to restore it, the mayor of Jerusalem at the time, Teddy Kollek, had offered to assist them with municipal city funding. But the Khalidis could not have accepted Israeli money to underwrite the project, given the tense political climate. Instead, they applied for and received grants from the Dutch government and the Ford Foundation, as the library was recognized as an important cultural treasure. Haifa Khalidi told me to try to imagine it as it had once been—with scaffolding on the walls and books in disrepair, gathering dust and withering away from lack of use.

At the entrance to the library, she pointed out a mausoleum, the burial site of Amir Husam ad-Din Barkah Khan and his two sons, who had fought against the Crusaders when they tried to conquer Jerusalem. In an adjacent room were family photos, including one of Ruhi Khalidi, with his dark hair brushed to one side and a carefully groomed mustache.

We ascended a narrow metal circular staircase to a small room where the most valuable parts of the collection and the microfilms were kept. As Haifa brought out document after document, I was able to conjure up the city as it had once been. Here was a 1798 letter written by an official in Jerusalem to the Sublime Porte, the seat of government in Constantinople, announcing the arrival in Palestine of "unbelievers," members of Napoleon's army who were attempting to conquer the Middle East. Another book described the last battle of Salah ad-Din and Richard the Lionhearted. Haifa carefully held out to me a four-hundred-year-old Koran with gilded pages and the royal blue emblem of the sultan, and then a book of hadith, or stories about the Koran, that she estimated was a thousand years old.

As she brought out each book, I hesitantly reached out to touch their covers, eager to feel history. The volumes were large and heavy, but the pages felt delicate, ephemeral, and I feared that they would disintegrate in my hands, the past that they contained turning to dust. My favorite was the six-hundred-year-old book that had been translated from Sanskrit to Persian and then into Arabic, containing everything the author knew about poisons and their various anti-dotes. This struck me as valuable information to possess, especially in a city of elaborate conflicts like Jerusalem.

Then Haifa Khalidi led me to a window and pulled back the cur-tains. She told me to look outside and asked, "What do you see there?" What I saw was a stairway that was so close that it nearly touched the panes of the window. The stairs led to a yeshiva, a reli-gious school for Jewish boys. It was likely one of the members of this very yeshiva whose murder had been commemorated in the graffiti on the wall I passed earlier in the day. The library and the yeshiva, both institutions devoted to the idea of learning, both valuing books above all and exalting the prominence of the written word, might have seemed to be the most natural of neighbors. It was quiet today; nothing stirred. But I knew that it had not always been that way.

2

In 1985, Shlomo Goren, Israel's chief rabbi from 1973 until 1983, opened a yeshiva in a building on Chain Street in the Jewish quarter of Jerusalem. The building had been purchased by an organization dedicated to buying properties and renovating them in areas they believed were once part of the ancient biblical City of David. The group was committed to establishing a Jewish presence on this site, and in addition to purchasing homes and settling Jews in them, in later years it helped sponsor archaeological exploration of the area as well, in the hope of further elucidating the Jewish historical connection to Jerusalem.

Rabbi Goren was one of the best-known rabbis in Israel, and not only because of his role as the former chief rabbi. In the heady days after the 1967 Arab-Israeli war, when it became clear that the Israeli army had not only captured biblically famous towns such as Bethlehem and Hebron in the West Bank but had also reunited the eastern and western halves of Jerusalem, a famous photo was taken that became an iconic symbol of that era. It featured Rabbi Goren standing on the Temple Mount, a traditional shofar, or ram's horn, to his lips, sounding out the ancient call of alarm, battle, and victory. For many Israelis, the photo presaged some of the most challenging issues that would arise in the wake of their return to the ancient sites, the heady mix of national and religious destiny and the questions they engendered, variations on some of the same issues that had troubled and perplexed people like Albert Antebi and Ruhi Khalidi over fifty years earlier.

The yeshiva that Rabbi Goren founded, Beit Idra, was an immediate success, as his illustrious name and status attracted students who wanted to study with him in the heart of ancient Jerusalem. The same group that had purchased the yeshiva building also bought a property across the street that they wanted to use as a dormitory for the students, who spent most of the day and night studying and needed a place where they could remain close to their teachers. Next to this dormitory was the Khalidi Library.

Not only were the Khalidi Library and the Goren yeshiva now neighbors, but because of the way the Old City was built, they actually pressed up against each other. When Haifa Khalidi looked out her window, she could see the stairs leading into the students' quarters. Parts of their building actually leaned on its porch.

In 1987, when the Khalidis decided to build a second floor onto their building as part of their renovation project to revitalize and then reopen the library to the public, the yeshiva went to court to get a restraining order preventing the construction. Even today, Haifa Khalidi remains bitter about the court case. "This had nothing to do with religion," she told me that June morning, sitting in the very room the family had gone to court to get built. "It has to do with human contact. It is about the relationship between us—how I treat them and how they treat me."

It took some time after that meeting with Haifa Khalidi to find a copy of the court's decision in the case, which was issued in 1988, but I eventually succeeded. I wanted to read the judge's opinion on this unusual dispute, and after doing so, I admired the court's ability to reach such a humane and nuanced decision. It is not always easy to separate a court from the times in which it adjudicates, and when this particular judgment was handed down, there was rioting and unrest in the West Bank. The first Palestinian intifada, a revolt in the West Bank and Gaza Strip against the Israeli occupation, had broken out not long before, and for the first time since Israel's capture of these territories in 1967, Israeli soldiers found themselves facing a full-scale revolt. Images of Palestinian youths with slingshots, throwing rocks at Israeli soldiers taking cover behind military jeeps, were everywhere. It must have been difficult for the judge to consider a dispute between two neighbors—one a prominent Palestinian Muslim family, the other a prominent Jewish rabbi—without seeing it in the context of the ongoing tumultuous political events.

And yet the court had tried to steer an evenhanded course. The judge in the case had even come to the site to assess the situation before issuing the ruling.

In the court's decision, the judge summarized the arguments that Beit Idra made in its request to stop its neighbor's building project. The yeshiva argued that when Khalidi family members were on the second floor of the library, they could see into the upper floor of the yeshiva's property. Not only would the addition to the library block the students' sun and light, but they did not feel safe being located in such close proximity. From the second floor of the library, it was a simple task to jump onto the porch of the building next door and gain entry. The students felt choked, the suit argued. They had to keep their doors and windows closed all the time because they feared their neighbors.

In the decision the court first ruled on the contention that the library blocked the students' sun and light. The judge felt that in a place as tightly constructed as the Old City, anytime someone changed or added to a structure, it was bound to have an impact on a neighbor. But in this case, she realized, this was not the heart of the issue. This wasn't a case about access to sun and light, but about security. It was about fear. The students feared their Arab neighbors.

"There is no doubt that a crowded building like that in the Old City and a mixed population between Jews and Arabs stirs up security fears," the judge wrote. The solution, however, was not to issue an overarching prohibition against any kind of building, but rather to address the fears and take protective steps. The judge quoted extensively from the testimony of two witnesses who spoke on behalf of the Khalidi family, Amnon Cohen and Dan Bahat, well-known Israeli Jewish academics. Cohen was a former high-ranking security officer who had worked in the West Bank. He had become a professor at Hebrew University and written seminal works about the Ottoman period. He was one of the first scholars to extensively mine the Islamic court records to reconstruct the life of Jews in Ottoman Jerusalem, and in fact, the courthouse was where Haifa Khalidi's father had first met him. "He had heard there was an Israeli, a Jew, at the Islamic courthouse every day," Amnon Cohen recounted to me. "He came over and introduced himself and asked me if I would like to see the family's library. Of course, I said yes." Dan Bahat was also a Hebrew University professor of archaeology. He worked as both an architect and an archaeologist, and in recent years had conducted digs under the auspices of the same group that had rented the building to Rabbi Goren's yeshiva.

Both men came to court to testify about the significance of the Khalidi Library. Cohen addressed the security issues raised by the yeshiva, and his background in the Israeli military apparently helped sway the court. He explained that the second-floor entry to the library would be locked, because that was where the family kept its most important historical documents and microfilms. The only people who would be allowed up there, he said, were academics, historians, and researchers, not the wider public. Bahat spoke about the architecture of the Old City. Virtually every building there was constructed so that the roofs touched one another or were so close that someone nimble could jump from roof to roof. It was possible for someone to take a walk around the neighborhood by leaping from roof to balcony to bedroom.

This was the nature of Jerusalem, the men argued. There was nothing unusual about the close proximity of the library and the yeshiva, or the uncertainty that arose when neighbors on opposite sides of a wider conflict ended up sharing space. Due to Jerusalem's unique history, people had lived this way for thousands of years and would continue to do so. It was therefore not sufficient for the yeshiva to argue that it would have less access to the sun. It was not sufficient to argue that its students were frightened. Overriding both these concerns was the larger idea, the message of the value of the history of Jerusalem.

The Khalidi Library was valuable not only because of the antiquity of its documents, and the historical events that they chronicled. The building and what it represented as part of the city's landscape had to be taken into account, as well. There was an entire history behind its founding and its development. Its story was of interest not only to the Khalidis, but to anyone who loved Jerusalem.

The court's decision was not particularly eloquent, but there was something inspiring in the fact that it chose not to judge this case as one involving the rights of a Jewish group versus the rights of a Muslim group. Instead, it viewed it as a case about maintaining a Jerusalem that had always been home to, and should always encompass, various diverse groups. There was value in the way the past shaped the city's present and future, and in finding a course to build a Jerusalem that could contain both a yeshiva and the Khalidi Library.

3

It had been a year since my visit to the library when in December 2005 I called Amnon Cohen in Jerusalem to speak to him about the case. Although the judge's ruling had permitted the renovations to continue, and the resulting library was a beautiful sanctuary, the violence that continued to grip Jerusalem in recent years meant that these days very few Israeli scholars ventured there. Dan Bahat still dropped by for coffee, Haifa Khalidi told me, but she said that even he had once worried aloud to her that his presence in her home at such a politically sensitive time might lead some of her neighbors or acquaintances to question her loyalty to the Palestinian cause, or perhaps even cause trouble for her. He had asked her if he should stop coming by for a time, at least until things quieted down. She had declined his offer, she said.

It struck me that Haifa Khalidi was stranded in a difficult place. She had told me that one of the values of the Khalidi Library was that "the Israelis say they came to a land with no people. This library shows there were people, and they were educated." But the Palestinian Authority, embroiled in so many seemingly intractable problems

of daily life, had not exactly embraced the library as a cultural resource. When I asked her about its relative neglect, Haifa replied
that the library was "not known" in Palestinian schools and left it at
that. But just as the street in Jerusalem named after Albert Antebi,
who had valued his ability to serve as a bridge between peoples, was
a dead end leading to nowhere, the library that Ruhi Khalidi had so
ardently championed was used in only a very limited way.

When I spoke with Amnon Cohen, he told me that only a few
days earlier he had been on the phone with Haifa Khalidi's brother,
who lives in Amman, Jordan. They were talking about the library
and the family's efforts to computerize it and create a Web site so
that scholars all over the world would not have to come to Jerusalem
to access its rich resources and unusual documents. With such tools,
the political climate would not stand in the way of scholarship, and
research and learning could go on. But the project was moving slowly.
Family members were scattered in different parts of the world, and
there were the inevitable political challenges. Still, the library's future seemed open.

Cohen said that the Khalidis had never forgotten his willingness
to testify on their behalf, and that he was always treated by them as
an honored member of the family. For his part, he felt that he had
done nothing special. He acknowledged that he held many political
views with which he was sure the Khalidi family would not agree,
and he added that he often had intense political disagreements about
Israeli policies with some of them. But despite this, he said the relationship was still mutually gratifying, and they were still able to
meet and talk as friends. "This is the real test," Cohen said. "When
people are willing to have tea or coffee together, do some gossiping,
and help out if need be, even if it's against their authority or their
authority's policies."

I listened to his words and realized why the modern story of the
library and the court's decision had so moved me. It reminded me of

another time, when Arabs and Jews could meet for coffee and see their fates as intertwined. It reminded me of Jerusalem in 1913.

Elizabeth Antebi, Albert Antebi's granddaughter, who had collected his letters from scattered archives and retraced the steps of his life while writing a biography of him, had described her grandfather to me as a "go-between," someone who was always wrestling with questions about the kind of brotherhood and connections that he shared with those around him. Once, in a letter to a friend who was urging him to join the Masonic temple in Jerusalem, he had declined, saying that he did not favor one brother over another, but rather saw himself as part of a broader humanity. When the sultan Abdul Hamid was deposed by the Young Turks in 1908, Antebi had climbed onto the balcony of a building near the Jaffa Gate of the Old City, in a spot that I had passed on my way to the Khalidi Library, and had helped throw two thousand loaves of bread into the crowd clamoring below in celebration. He had seen himself as a man of his time, at home wherever he went in the city.

One of the incidents that had sparked Elizabeth Antebi's quest into her family's past had been a folder filled with documents and photos that one of her cousins had given her. Among them were the papers written in a nearly illegible scrawl by Antebi that outlined his vision of Palestine's ultimately being divided into a series of ethnic cantons. In the end, he had remained unwilling to fully embrace either Arab or Jewish nationalism. Instead, Elizabeth Antebi argued, he had held out for a notion that she described as "ideals are better than ideologies." That struck me as being the same message the Khalidi Library had embraced.

But everywhere in Jerusalem now, ideologies had taken over. When Elizabeth Antebi reflected on her grandfather's legacy, she knew that the Jerusalem that he loved, and the wider world that he had once inhabited, were no more. "The Arabs of those days are no more the Arabs of today," she wrote me, "especially with the question of Hamas" and other radical Islamic groups that did not believe in any sort of compromise with Israel.

After Antebi was banished from Jerusalem, he never returned. The years of hardship during the war, and his anger over his exile from Palestine, led him to write to a friend about his years in the city, "I lament the sacrifice of my life and regret being bound to a land that devours me." He was alluding to a well-known biblical story, in the book of Numbers, which recounts how Moses sent out spies as an advance party to the Promised Land. They brought back a negative report, telling Moses that it would be impossible to attack the people already living there and expect to win because they were stronger than the Israelites. "The land we explored devours those living in it," they claimed.

Even now, though, it was hard to abandon the appeal and value of the role of the go-between, of people like Ruhi Khalidi and Albert Antebi who straddled different worlds and were sometimes devoured in the process. When I started writing this book, I wanted to better understand how we had arrived today at such a violent impasse, and the events of 1913 and beyond had shown me the path that had taken us to that point. I shared Elizabeth Antebi's assessment that her grandfather's most important legacy was a kind of pragmatism about the limits of ideology. It has taken Israel decades to finally reach the same conclusion. Now the very things that Antebi had predicted to his Zionist friends back in 1913—especially his concern that Jews could not maintain a demographic majority indefinitely in Palestine—were being debated by Israeli politicians, researchers, thinkers, and leaders.

The warning that Antebi had presciently sounded had been ignored for too long, but social, geographic, and demographic realities cannot easily be overcome, no matter how much someone wants it or wills it to be so. While Antebi's specific political proposal no longer had relevance to the current situation in the Middle East—

his document had been written during another era and under unique political circumstances—that wasn't the same thing as saying his ideals represented a dead end.

To go in search of the Ottoman past and Antebi's place in it was to believe that while the issues confronting Jerusalem are and have always been very difficult and painful, there was a basis for resolving them. "Of course we cannot say really that Albert won for now," Elizabeth Antebi had written to me from her home in Paris, and it is easy to imagine her grandfather agreeing with her pragmatic assessment. "But why not once?"

4

One day in 2006 I noticed a small news item in the Israeli newspaper *Haaretz*. Turkey had just announced that it had transferred to the Palestinian Authority an enormous Ottoman archive, comprising some 14,000 pages of documents about Jerusalem and Palestine dating from the period beginning in 1500 and ending in 1914. The archive apparently contained records and information about land deals and land purchases that would be relevant in Jerusalem today. It wasn't clear yet what the archive would reveal, but the shadow cast by 1913 seemed to loom ever larger over the city's future.

There were other points of connection linking that era to today. Jerusalem was once again on the cusp of enormous change, driven by political forces that could not be easily controlled. Deferring a discussion about the future of the city had been one of the first topics the Israelis and Palestinians had agreed upon when they first started talks that led to the signing of the Oslo peace agreement in

1993. But postponing a debate over the resolution of that subject no longer seemed possible.

Jerusalem has always been at the heart of the ongoing Arab-Israeli political dispute. The Palestinian Authority's pronouncements and Israel's policies and settlement activities have typically been made with one eye turned toward their impact on Jerusalem. Settlements were built, a wall was constructed, lines were drawn in the West Bank, all with an underlying conception of how they might reinforce or strengthen Jerusalem.

But postponing a discussion of the city's political future has created other dire consequences. Jerusalem has been buckling under the enormous weight of the continuing inability of the opposing sides not so much to fail to come to a final agreement—which seemed years off—as to fail even to talk openly about any aspect of the city's future. Recently it has sunk slowly into poverty and disrepair. Politicians are ready to call Jerusalem the "eternal capital" of Israel but do not seem sufficiently alarmed that for years more Israelis have left Jerusalem than have moved there. There are few jobs available for young Israelis who grew up in the city, housing is unaffordable, and the beauty of the downtown area is fading as the increasing number of people living in poverty overwhelm the infrastructure.

Haim Ramon, an Israeli politician, told the press in an interview in December 2005, as Israel embarked on an election campaign, that he feared for the city. Jerusalem, he said, could end up becoming "the non-Jewish and non-Zionist capital of Israel," referring to the growing number of ultrareligious Jews and Palestinian Arabs in the city, neither of whom identified with the state. Because the borders of the city have been expanded far beyond what would have been recognizable to Albert Antebi or Ruhi Khalidi in 1913, Israel's Jewish demographic control is now in danger. Out of the larger city's population today of 650,000, one in three people is a Palestinian Arab. The Old

City, where Antebi and Khalidi once lived side by side, and where the sites with the deepest national and religious significance to the different ethnic communities are located, is now home to approximately 32,000 Arabs and only 4,000 Jews, according to government statistics published by the Israeli press.

There is constant political rhetoric by both sides but no c
ling vision for how to revitalize Jerusalem. At the Jerusal
tute for Israel Studies, a team of Israeli researchers ha:
grapple with some of these challenges, working for years
potential scenarios on how to resolve the city's issues. /
proposals were an exchange of territories so that both t
and the Arab sides would have control over congruent ter:
an Israeli recognition of Palestinian sovereignty over all ‹
rusalem other than Jewish neighborhoods and parts of the ᴜ₁ᴜ ᴄ₁.ᵧ.
Other ideas were floated in the press; still others remained frozen in papers and memos. But there was no shortage of creative solutions.

In a book published in 2005 called *The Jerusalem Lexicon* by researchers at the Institute, the geographer Shlomo Hasson articulated what had become clear to most people who studied the problem of Jerusalem's future. "The existence of a democratic state and the continuation of Jewish hegemony in Jerusalem necessitate getting out of the existing situation and adopting new solutions," Hasson wrote. "Above all it is desirable to separate the space in which Jews live from the space where Arabs live and for each side to have the most sovereignty in its area." This is where things had led, from 1913 to our own time—back to the idea of a separate peace.

5

Over the years of reporting and writing this book, I grew to admire much about the inhabitants of Jerusalem in 1913—their pragmatism, their resilience, their willingness to express their fears. Among these remarkable individuals, the one who perhaps most engaged me, though, was Arthur Ruppin. Some of the interest was personal, certainly, as my own sojourn in the Middle East had started in a Hebrew class, and I found his attempts to learn Hebrew, despite the ever-present German accent that always gave his origins away, reminiscent of my own efforts. I also appreciated the way he was willing to laugh at his own linguistic foibles. He admitted in his journal that at a wedding that he and his wife attended in Tel Aviv in 1936, he "committed the howler of the evening," by introducing the hostess of the wedding as "the woman who sleeps next to me," instead of "the woman who sits next to me." (Moreover, in modern Hebrew, the word Ruppin used for "sleeps" was also used to imply a sexual relationship.) "Nevertheless," he concluded after the event in his understated way, "I decided to make no more Hebrew after-dinner speeches."

I had also found many of the things he wrote especially relevant to the current problems in Jerusalem. Unlike Albert Antebi or Ruhi Khalidi, who were both dead by the time the British Mandate officially started in 1920 in Palestine, Arthur Ruppin had been fortunate to live a long life and had the benefit of being able to refine his political views in response to changing circumstances. In 1913, he had sounded audacious when he told the delegates to the Zionist

Congress that they should attempt to become the majority in Palestine. The victory of his ideas had forced him to look differently at the situation.

It had taken others in the Zionist movement decades after the founding of Israel to come to the same conclusions that Ruppin had reached long before Israel was even a state—that what the Zionists perceived as the advantages of their presence in Palestine would not move the Arab side to give up their own ideological positions. And he had understood in 1913 what Israeli politicians have publicly started articulating only in the past few years—namely, that the notion of a Jewish state meant nothing if there was not a Jewish majority living in that state.

Included in a collection of Ruppin's diaries was an afterword, an English translation of a 1968 speech given by then Israeli defense minister Moshe Dayan to the graduates of the Israeli army's command and staff school. Could there have been two men more different in style, temperament, or personality than Arthur Ruppin and Moshe Dayan? Dayan, the dashing war hero with the black patch over the eye he lost in combat, a native-born Israeli, with his roguish humor, his earthy, coarse Hebrew peppered with army slang; and Arthur Ruppin, the technocrat, primary architect of the drive to obtain land in Palestine, the German immigrant and maker of hapless after-dinner speeches in mangled Hebrew.

I found it fascinating that, in a speech given a little over a year after Israel's stunning victory in the 1967 war, Dayan had chosen to offer an appreciation of Arthur Ruppin. In the wake of that war, as it happened, Dayan was thinking not so much about peace as "the problematics of peace," a phrase of which Ruppin himself might have approved. Wasn't that what had always been at the very heart of the issue, from the time the Zionist movement started right up until our own era?

In his own version of considering the "problematics of peace,"

Arthur Ruppin had touched on every relevant issue: The dilemma of pushing for majority rule in Palestine. The virtual certainty that such a course would eventually lead to war and the loss of life. His fear of terrorism from the Arabs. His concern that the constant struggle for survival might result in violence on the Jewish side. Dayan had quoted Ruppin's raising of his own internal doubts about the path down which his vision seemed inexorably to lead. Ruppin felt depressed when he thought about how to balance the realization of Zionism with what he referred to as "general ethical considerations." "Is Zionism really to end up as shallow chauvinism?" he had lamented in his journal. "Is it impossible to provide the ever growing number of Jews in Palestine with a field of activity without oppressing the Arabs?"

Ruppin, Dayan argued, had eventually "stopped dealing with the 'Arab question' because he realized that the Arabs would not agree to Zionism," even if it brought prosperity and progress to the land. He concluded his talk by reading aloud an entry from Ruppin's diary in 1936, the year during which Arab nationalist riots exploded in Jerusalem and other areas of Palestine. Many people died in those riots, and the loss of life and the ongoing state of war between the two groups was unfortunately inevitable, Ruppin had written. If we want to continue our work in Palestine, he had added, such loss of life is a tragic reality that must be borne.

Dayan had chosen this idea as his conclusion probably because it suited his own frame of mind at the time. He viewed the conquest of the West Bank, the Gaza Strip, and even Jerusalem as a complex legacy, one that he knew Israel would grapple with for years to come, and for which a heavy loss of life had already been the price. But when I reflected on his speech and his observations about Ruppin's views about war and peace, I felt almost certain that Ruppin himself would have chosen a different entry as a more fitting conclusion.

Dayan had written his speech thirty-two years after Ruppin made that journal entry. Today, I write these words thirty-eight years after Dayan's speech, and the issues have not changed much for either of us since Ruppin set them out. But in wrestling with the invariable "problematics of peace," I disagree with Dayan's emphasis on Ruppin's apparent acceptance of a state of constant violence, his apparent coming to terms with the steady, inexorable loss of life.

Instead, I prefer remarks that Ruppin recorded in Jerusalem a year later, in 1937, when he considered the compromise that had just been proposed by the British, to divide Palestine into Jewish and Arab parts, one of the many attempts that were made over the next decades to find a way for the two sides to resolve their conflict and live in peace. Ruppin cast his eyes on all that had happened. Perhaps he thought about his speech to the Zionist Congress in 1913 championing the push for a Jewish majority in Palestine, and the many achievements and setbacks, victories and losses of life that had followed. It had been a long road to get to this moment. The compromise the British proposed did not represent all that he had wanted, dreamed about, worked toward. The choices that lay before him were painful. He knew that the idea of relinquishing any part of Palestine would be viewed by many Jews, including himself, "as a serious loss," and he felt that potential loss sharply. Despite it all, though, he had still concluded, "It is not, however, a question of what we *would like* but of what we *can have*." (The emphasis is his.) Wherever I walked in Jerusalem, those words seemed as haunting and relevant for both the Arabs and the Israelis today as they were back then.

Acknowledgments

I'm grateful to Edward Felsenthal, Eben Shapiro, and Hilary Stout of *The Wall Street Journal*, for their friendship and support of this project.

My agent, Kris Dahl, saw the story in Jerusalem and pushed others to see it, too. My editor at Viking Penguin, Rick Kot, brought a judicious eye, a gift for detail, and a love of storytelling to every line of the book. I know he would be welcome at any table in a Jerusalem café.

My parents, Bob and Golda Dockser, were a constant source of love and support. They were the ones who first took me to Jerusalem and showed me why they loved the city. Every corner I turn there reminds me of happy times spent with them and my sister, Lynne. I'm grateful to my husband, Ronen Marcus, who endured my odd writing hours and tendency to create stacks of documents everywhere in our house. There is no one I would rather have by my side, in Jerusalem or anywhere else in the world.

In relying so extensively on letters, diaries, and archival material, I depended on a number of translators to make sure I understood what I was reading. Ahmad Jabari translated the Arabic documents and helped me understand the context in which they were written. Lisa Harris-Schumann made the 1913 Zionist Congress come alive with her deft translation of the German. Neil Hubacker translated the Antebi letters and other documents in French. Salim Tamari, who is helping spearhead the publication of both Wasif Jawhariyyeh's memoirs and a new Arabic edition of Khalil Sakakini's diaries, shared early versions of his papers and research on the men as well as available English translations. His effort to better understand the past is inspiring and I appreciated his generosity in sharing the wealth of his knowledge. Nancy Shekter-Porat was indefatigable in tracking down obscure documents in libraries, offices, and archives around Israel, but I am most grateful for her warm friendship.

Walid Khalidi and Rashid Khalidi both spent time with me discussing their research into the Khalidi family and the Middle East. Walid Khalidi provided me with portions of Ruhi's unpublished manuscript on Zionism, as well as other helpful documents. Both Walid and Rashid arranged for me to visit the family library in Jerusalem, one of the city's many unsung treasures, and I am grateful for Haifa Khalidi's willingness to show me around and share some of its history.

Elizabeth Antebi was incredibly helpful throughout the course of this project. She shared her huge cache of Antebi letters that she had collected from archives around the world, along with family papers. She sent me the as yet unpublished English translation of her remarkable French biography of her grandfather, and introduced me to members of the Antebi family still living in Israel. I am truly the beneficiary of her groundbreaking scholarship in providing an alternative narrative of this era.

Finally, to my children, Eden and Yuval, a mother's love and gratitude for your presence in my life, and a quiet prayer: May you always feel at home in Jerusalem.

Notes on Sources

In trying to reconstruct a narrative of a contentious time period that reflects many different voices, I encountered numerous difficulties. For one thing, far more original documents and letters were available to me from members of the Zionist movement than from those who participated in the nascent Palestinian nationalist movement.

At least initially, the Zionist leaders were dispersed between Germany, Palestine, and Turkey, and so there was extensive correspondence among them as they tried to keep up the daily business of coordinating their burgeoning political movement. Moreover, once the state of Israel was founded in 1948, there was a central government actively interested in preserving these documents. A visitor to Jerusalem today has very little trouble digging up decades of history.

It was far more challenging for me to find Arabic documents reflecting the Palestinian perspective from these same years. This is partly due to the dispersion of many Palestinian intellectuals in the years after the wars in 1948 and 1967, the enormous dislocation this engendered, and the loss of private documents as people moved around. Many of the countries where Palestinians ended up were repressive and did not create conditions that allowed for the publication of diaries and letters. When material did get published, it was sometimes edited by loved ones, colleagues, or friends of the writer, who for political or emotional reasons sometimes did not want to include all the material. To this day, many important personal papers remain unpublished, maintained in private family archives. They are only available if a scholar first knows where to find them and, even then, only if the family is interested in sharing and publishing them.

This situation is starting to change, mainly due to the coming of age of a new generation of Israeli and Palestinian scholars who share a greater interest in looking openly at the past, a willingness to ask critical questions about the actions and decisions of their political leaders, and a sense of urgency about the importance of this effort. In writing this book, I have been the beneficiary of some of this early work, and I anticipate that in the coming years more diaries and journals will be published, new documents will come to light, and engaging histories that offer multiple perspectives on the past will emerge. I believe that our appreciation of this crucial period in Middle Eastern history, and the way it continues to shape our present, will only deepen.

Introduction: Jerusalem 2004–2006

I purchased a videotape of *The Life of the Jews in Palestine* from the Israel Broadcasting Authority, and viewed it numerous times. Even without any voices, the images themselves were riveting as they so vividly captured a lost part of history. An interesting discussion about the image of Arab laborers in Zionist photography and films of this era can be found in Michael Berkowitz's *Zionist Culture and West European Jewry Before the First World War*, pp. 149–152.

I relied extensively on Arthur Ruppin's journals and letters collected and edited by Alex Bein, *Arthur Ruppin: Memoirs, Diaries, Letters*. Ruppin's comments about his 1913 speech and his wariness about participating in the 1913 Zionist Congress can be found in the collection on pp. 146–149.

The growing interest in the Ottoman era has been expressed most prominently in archaeology, where political goals and scientific questions are often intertwined. Given how important biblical archaeology has been to Israel and Israelis, it is perhaps not surprising that the Palestinians would try to mine the Ottoman era, the period right before the start of the British Mandate that ended in the creation of modern Israel, for insights into the development of Palestinian national identity. Some of the current reexamination of the history of the era by scholars is, in my opinion, at least partially the result of the groundwork laid by archaeologists and archaeology historians. Neil Asher Silberman wrote an illuminating account of his visit to the David's Citadel gift shop in his *Between Past and Present*, pp. 233–237, and interesting insights about the use of the Ottoman past in the ongoing political struggle in the Middle East are also recounted in Uzi Baram and Lynda Carroll's introduction, "The Future of the Ottoman Past," in their book *A Historical Archaeology of the Ottoman Empire*, which expertly draws together some of the latest results and thinking about that period. Ghada Ziadeh-Seely called for a new approach to Palestinian archaeology as far back as 1987 in an article that ran in *Bir Zeit Research News* called "The

Present Is Our Key to the Past," and then supplied a cogent summary of the Palestinian expedition's more recent findings at the city of Ti'innik in the Baram and Carroll book, pp. 79–91. Another important paper that focused renewed attention on the Ottoman era was Beshara Doumani's "Rediscovering Ottoman Palestine" in the *Journal of Palestine Studies*, Winter 1992.

Part One: Jerusalem 1898

In recent years, much has been written about Theodor Herzl, and I mined biographies about him by Alex Bein, Amos Elon, and Ernst Pawel for information about his life and times. Herzl was a voluminous record-keeper; he filled notebook after notebook recounting his efforts to get people to pay attention to his ideas for a Jewish state. His diaries, edited by Martin Lowenthal, were an important source of information for his thoughts and reactions during his trip to Jerusalem. But one of the most important resources about Herzl's time in Palestine is a book that has received less attention, called *Im Herzl Li-Yerushaliyim (With Herzl to Jerusalem)*, written in Hebrew and based on an exhibition of documents and pictures at the Central Zionist Archives in Jerusalem. More information about the exhibition and some of the pictures from it can be found on the CZA's Web site, www.zionistarchives.org.il. The request by Herzl's wife, Julia, for a pair of slippers as a souvenir from what he saw as one of the most momentous political journeys of his life was mentioned in that book. Her mundane request summed up for me the huge gap between the couple in the way they viewed Herzl's mission.

I never tire of reading memoirs about life in Jerusalem, whether they concern the modern era, such as Lesley Hazelton's *Jerusalem, Jerusalem: A Memoir of Love and Peace*, Bertha Spafford Vester's chatty and somewhat quaint recounting of her family's life in Ottoman-era Jerusalem, *Our Jerusalem: An American Family in the Holy City,* or the many books about Palestine and Jerusalem by James Finn, who served as the British consul in the city from 1846 to 1863, and his even more prolific wife, Elizabeth Finn. But the memoirs I enjoyed most, and relied on most heavily for my reconstruction of Jerusalem in the years leading up to World War I, were those of Jacob Yehoshua, especially *Jerusalem in Days of Old*. His books are written in Hebrew, but in their loving reconstruction of life in that city, and their detailed and evocative portrait of a relationship between Jews and Muslims that today seems hard to imagine, they are well worth reading and merit a much wider audience than they have so far enjoyed.

The Khalidi family is one of the best known in Jerusalem, and the exchange of letters between Herzl and Yusuf Khalidi has been written about many times, including in Benny Morris's *Righteous Victims*, Neville J. Mandel's seminal work *The Arabs and Zionism Before World War I*, and Rashid Khalidi's *Palestinian Identity*, which contains the most comprehensive information about both Yusuf and Ruhi Khalidi and has the benefit of being able to tap into Rashid's interviews with his family. Walid Khalidi was kind enough to share with me portions of Ruhi Khalidi's unpublished work, *Zionism or the Zionist Question*, as well as his analysis of the book in an article in Arabic, "The book 'Zionism or the Zionist Question' by Muhammad Ruhi al-Khalidi, died 1913." The book has never been published in English and I relied on a translation into English that was made for me by Ahmad Jabari.

Albert Antebi, long forgotten by most Israelis today, has enjoyed a resurgence of interest by scholars interested in the pre–World War I era, thanks to the amazing work done by his granddaughter, Elizabeth Antebi, in researching his life. Her biography of Albert Antebi, *L'homme du serail*, has been published in French only, but Elizabeth provided me with an English translation that has been made and will hopefully be published someday. Her Web site, www.antebiel.com, is a remarkable resource for any scholar interested in this period because she has made available to anyone who is interested a cache of letters written by Albert Antebi that are stored in archives in France and in Israel. These letters served as the basis for her dissertation on Antebi, and were a key source for me in reconstructing Antebi's experiences in Jerusalem during this period. They eloquently capture in his own words his mounting anger and sadness at the emerging political conflict between Zionists and Arabs in the city. Antebi is a poignant figure because he tried to straddle multiple worlds and identities and ultimately was forced to choose sides. He was an incredibly prolific letter writer, which makes his letters an important resource of this period, but it is his astute political analysis of the events of his time that makes reading his letters so fascinating. Many of the issues he raised, and the conclusions that he drew, have proven accurate in our own time.

Part Two: Jerusalem 1908

The rise of the Young Turks to power in the Ottoman Empire had a huge effect on life in Jerusalem, fully unleashing for the first time the forces of nationalism. The elections that sent Ruhi Khalidi to the newly reconstituted Ottoman Parliament brought the Zionist-Arab conflict to a more public platform. Khalidi's speech to Parliament in 1911, and the repercussions it had back home in Jerusalem, is covered in many sources, including Rashid Khalidi's *Palestinian Identity*, Michelle Ursula Campos's unpublished dissertation "'Shared Homeland' and Its Boundaries," Neville J. Mandel's *The Arabs and Zionism*, and Aharon Cohen's masterful *Israel and the Arab World*. I was also able to find contemporary newspaper accounts of the celebration in Jerusalem of the rise to power of the Young Turks in a November 17, 1908, issue of the Hebrew newspaper *ha-Zvi*. My analysis of Ruhi Khalidi's evolving attitude toward Zionism is based on the observations he makes in his unpublished *Zionism* manuscript.

In this chapter, I relied on the following Antebi letters, all from Elizabeth Antebi's collection of archival material: 191, 295, 117, 118, 283, 325, 310, 359, and 461.

One of the most interesting and important collections of letters from this era is the result of David Kushner's work on the former governor of Jerusalem, Ali Ekrem. For an Ottoman view of the nascent Zionist-Arab conflict I not only depended on Ekrem's letters, which Kushner collected and translated into Hebrew in *Moshel Hayiti bi-Yerushaliyim*, but enjoyed reading his writing in tandem with his daughter Selma's memoir in English, *Unveiled*, which recounts some of the same episodes from the perspective of a young woman and devoted daughter. For someone who spent only two years in Jerusalem, Ali Ekrem managed to write numerous letters. His disdain for both the Jews and the Arabs comes through in his writing; he did not enjoy his time in Jerusalem and seemed to take the "pox on both your houses" approach to governing. He comes across in many of his letters as a vain and touchy man, but his warning that the conflict in Jerusalem was eventually going to end in violence—words that were apparently ignored and somewhat ridiculed by his colleagues back in Constantinople—today seems prescient.

Part Three: Jerusalem 1913

The poem that appears in the epigraph of the chapter appears in Mandel's *Arabs and Zionism*.

The documents and reports sent by various Zionist officials back to the Zionist Action Committee in Berlin were an important resource for me. They can all be found in the Central Zionist Archives in Jerusalem. Most are written in German, and I had the documents translated by Lisa Harris-Schumann. Her translation of the massive protocols from the 1913 Zionist Congress, the last meeting held before the outbreak of World War I, was critical in my recounting of the key debates that took place.

The system of land purchases in Palestine and its role in the ongoing Israeli-Palestinian conflict can be found in Gershon Shafir's *Land, Labor and the Origins of the Israeli-Palestinian Conflict*. Ruhi Khalidi's own analysis of the role Jewish land purchases played in the ascendancy of the Zionist movement is based on his writing in the *Zionism* manuscript. Campos's "'Shared Homeland'" has an extensive history of the split among the members of the Masonic lodge in Jerusalem.

The incident at Rehovot in 1913 is barely known today, and yet it loomed large for many of the characters in this book. A recounting of the events can be found in two reports that were sent in 1913 to the Action Committee of the Zionist Organization in Berlin, which are available at the Central Zionist Archives in Jerusalem. When I went to the archive in search of documents about the Rehovot dispute, I was amazed to find a whole folder filled with letters and documents. There was extensive correspondence between the Zionist representatives in Palestine and officials back in Europe. Albert Antebi wrote about the incident in his letters, particularly letter 471, because he was eventually called in to act as an intermediary between the Jewish settlers and the Ottoman government. This is also a good illustration of the many ways that Antebi, a self-described anti-Zionist, found himself working more closely with the Zionist movement as the years went by. He felt loyalty to all Jews in distress, no matter what their political affiliations might be, but he also recognized that any conflict between Zionists and Arabs was bound to have repercussions for the entire Jewish community in Palestine. He worried that the Zionist leaders' lack of experience living with Arabs, and their misunderstanding of Arab culture, would result in serious problems. The Rehovot incident only confirmed his dire view of the political inexperience of the Zionist leadership in Palestine.

One of the most fascinating accounts of what happened at Rehovot in 1913 can be found in dueling articles that ran in *Filastin*, an Arabic newspaper. The Jewish and Arab authors of the two articles offered completely different interpretations of the events. It is one of the earliest examples of how almost from the very beginning of the national conflict, the two sides could not agree on a common narrative, a problem that continues to plague them even today.

The descriptions in this chapter of life in Jerusalem during this period come mainly from Jacob Yehoshua's books and also the memoirs of Wasif Jawhariyyeh, a Christian Arab, who as a musician playing at the many parties around the city got to know a wide range of characters. Some portions of his memoirs appeared in English translation in several issues of the *Jerusalem Quarterly File*. Other sections I had translated from the Arabic by Ahmad Jabari. Three volumes of the memoirs are being published in Arabic as *Oud wa Barood: The Jerusalem Diaries of Wasif Jawhariyyeh (1904–1948)*, edited by Issam Nassar and Salim Tamari. Tamari is also the editor of the *Jerusalem Quarterly File*.

The 1913 peace negotiations were one of the first of many attempts to resolve the Arab-Israeli conflict, in particular the Palestinian-Israeli conflict. In reconstructing the negotiations, I relied on the work of Mandel, Cohen, and Neil Caplan's *Futile Diplomacy*, the title of which sums up much of the history of these negotiations. But the main source for the chronicle are the letters and reports of Victor Jacobson and Sami Hochberg, whose role was similar to the one played by the Israeli academics who started talks with their Palestinian counterparts that eventually resulted in the 1993 Oslo peace accords. Hochberg was friends with all the Zionist leaders but not one himself, and so if he agreed to something the others did not support he could be easily disavowed. Hochberg was probably among the few, if not the only, Jews to attend the Arab-Syrian National Congress in Paris. His reports and Jacobson's analysis of the situation can all be found in the Central Zionist Archives. Most of the material was written in German or French, and a translation was provided for me by Neil Hubacker and Lisa Harris-Schumann. The files I consulted at the archives are: L2-26: L2-34-11; L569; Z3752; Z3114; Z3115; Z345; Z347; Z365; Z31456; Z3114. One of the best reconstructions of the conference itself appears in Eliezer Tauber's *The Emergence of the Arab Movements*, pp. 178–212.

The 1914 negotiations, which were unsuccessful but did not formally break down until the outbreak of World War I, were reconstructed from the Cohen, Caplan, and Mandel texts. I also relied on letters sent by Ruppin, Jacobson, and Richard Lichtheim, among others, who were all personally involved in the negotiations, and whose documents are found in the Central Zionist Archives. Mandel, p. 213, is the source for the "armed gangs" quote.

Part Four: Jerusalem 1914

The Yehuda Amichai epigraph that opens the chapter is from his poem "Seven Laments for the War Dead." His poems capture the many dilemmas of life in Jerusalem.

The memoirs of Arthur Ruppin and Wasif Jawhariyyeh were critical in my understanding of this period. Salim Tamari not only published many selections of the journal in the *Jerusalem Quarterly File*, but also wrote an interesting article about the importance of Jawhariyyeh's memoirs called "A Musician's Lot: The Jawhariyyeh Memoirs as a Key to the Early Modernity of Jerusalem." He sent me many of his papers about Jawhariyyeh and other important Jerusalem figures of this era prior to their publication.

I also used Sakakini's journals as an important source. His diaries were translated many years ago into Hebrew under the title *Kazeh Ani Olam* (*Such Am I, O World*), and it is that translation which I mainly relied upon in this chapter. A new Arabic edition of Sakakini's diaries is starting to appear, the work of Salim Tamari and his colleagues. Sakakini's daughter, who edited the version of the diary that was translated into Hebrew, apparently removed a number of the entries out of concern that they were politically inappropriate or due to personal sensitivities about how her father might be perceived. Tamari and his colleagues are publishing a complete, unabridged version of the journals in several volumes. They have also started translating some of the entries into English. "Khalil Sakakini's Ottoman Prison Diaries," which ran in the January 2004 issue of the *Jerusalem Quarterly File*, was a moving document and enhances our understanding of the complexity of Sakakini's relationships with Jews, including those who played a role in the creation of Israel. Some of Sakakini's most interesting conversations about Zionism took place during the Arabic lessons he gave to Jews in Jerusalem who were prominent in the effort to purchase land for Jewish settlement.

The way that the current political dispute sometimes impacts the way events in the past are remembered or presented to the public can be seen in Ruhi Khalidi's history as well. There were rumors that Ruhi, who died in Constantinople in 1913, was poisoned because of his anti-Zionist activities, perhaps even due to what he was writing in his book on Zionism that was still not completed at the time of his death. Rashid Khalidi, a descendant of Ruhi, prolific Middle Eastern historian and head of the Middle Eastern Studies Department at Columbia University in New York City, attempted to trace the source of this rumor and speculated that it may have arisen at a time of nationalist fervor in Jerusalem in the 1920s. Interviewing some of his family members who had lived through this period, Rashid told me that after conducting his interviews he had concluded that in all likelihood Ruhi had in fact died of disease that was rampant at that time throughout the empire, and that theories and rumors casting his death in a more nationalist light or as somehow connected to the Arab-Israeli dispute had been put forth because they better suited the nationalist spirit of later times.

All of the Antebi letters cited in this chapter can be found in the collection compiled by Elizabeth Antebi. I used letters 494, 507, 509, Appendix A in this chapter.

The British Mandate period in Palestine has resulted in its own rich collection of works, of both scholarship and fiction. In the fiction category, *Mandelbaum Gate* by Muriel Spark, *When I Lived in Modern Times* by Linda Grant, and *A Palestine Affair* by Jonathan Wilson are all wonderful books that bring to life a city where spies, eccentrics, poets, and nationalists all turned up at the same parties and at the same coffee houses. A. J. Sherman's *Mandate Days* taps into the rich collection of papers, letters, and diaries written by British officers and soldiers who served in Palestine during this period. Tom Segev's *One Palestine, Complete* is a compelling read, and makes the provocative argument that the Palestinians, rather than the Israelis, were actually the underdogs in the 1948 war that led to Israel's creation. To get a feel for how the British physically changed Jerusalem during this period, see David Kroyanker's *Jerusalem Architecture*. It was the British governor of Jerusalem who put into effect the edict still in force today that all construction in the city must be done with the local limestone that gives Jerusalem its distinctive and beautiful physical look.

Epilogue: Jerusalem 2004–2006

The Khalidi Library is one of the delights of Jerusalem, but is off the beaten track for most visitors to the city. Rashid and Walid Khalidi arranged with their cousin Haifa Khalidi, the current family caretaker of the library, to meet with me there. She spent time with me recounting its history, and told me about the legal case between the library and Rabbi Goren's yeshiva. I was able to track down a copy of the decision thanks to Elias Khoury, the family's lawyer, and the persistence of my friend Nancy Shekter-Porat. I am also grateful to Amnon Cohen, who testified on behalf of the Khalidi family and shared his thoughts about its significance with me. The decision's case number is T.A. 174/88. I translated it from the Hebrew.

I probably would have walked by the library had I not been accompanied by Abigail Jacobson, an Israeli scholar, delightful Jerusalem walking companion, and one of Rashid Khalidi's graduate students. Abigail is working on a dissertation set in the Ottoman period, and based on her research she has published a number of fascinating articles about the Sephardic Jewish community in the pre–World War I era and their interactions with their Arab neighbors, including an August 2004 piece in the *Jerusalem Quarterly File* that I especially liked called "Alternative Voices in Late Ottoman Palestine." In reading her work, it is hard not to draw the conclusion that she believes that had Sephardic Jews like Albert Antebi—who spoke Arabic, felt at home in Arabic culture, and wanted to remain integrated with their Arab neighbors even as they sought greater Jewish autonomy—wielded more cultural and political influence in shaping the early direction of Israel's relationship with the Arab world, the outcome might have been different than it was, and possibly better.

Elizabeth Antebi, Albert's granddaughter, shared her thoughts about her grandfather's legacy with me, as well as private family papers related to him such as a letter from David Ben-Gurion, the first prime minister of Israel. Ben-Gurion recounted in the letter that when he was jailed and ultimately exiled from Palestine for his Zionist activities, Albert Antebi was the only one with the courage to come visit him in jail, a humane gesture that Ben-Gurion never forgot and greatly admired. Antebi has a street named after him in Jerusalem; it is a dead end, something that I think Antebi might have found amusing or, at the least, fodder for a rant in one of his letters, had he lived to see it.

The subject of Jerusalem's future routinely comes up whenever there is an Israeli election. Haim Ramon's quote about his fears that Jerusalem is becoming a non-Jewish and non-Zionist capital appeared in a *Haaretz* article on December 15, 2005. There are quieter efforts under way to plan for Jerusalem's future. *The Jerusalem Lexicon*, a book published in 2005, details some of the research and emerging thinking. Given the election of Hamas officials to the Palestinian Authority and that party's refusal to recognize Israel's right to exist or to honor previous commitments made by the Palestinian Authority in negotiations with Israel, it seems unlikely that there will be public discussions about Jerusalem's future anytime soon. But one of my conclusions from my research is that what made the Antebis, Ruppins, Sakakinis, and Khalidis of Jerusalem so fascinating is that they were always thinking and strategizing about the city's future, no matter what was happening in the present, and were working to find a way to strengthen the city that they loved.

Bibliography

Aaronsohn, Alexander. *With the Turks in Palestine*. Boston and New York: Houghton Mifflin Company, 1916.

Abu-Lughod Ibrahim, ed. *Transformation of Palestine*. Evanston, IL: Northwestern University Press, 1987.

Agnon, S. Y. *Only Yesterday*. Princeton, NJ: Princeton University Press, 2000.

Al-Jubeh, Nazmi. "Libraries and Archives: The Khalidiyah Library." *Jerusalem Quarterly File* 3 (1999).

Amichai, Yehuda. *Amen*. New York: Harper & Row, 1977.

———. *The Selected Poetry of Yehuda Amichai*. Berkeley and Los Angeles: University of California Press, 1996.

Antebi, Elizabeth. "Albert Antebi or The Religion of France: Letters." Dissertation. Ecole Pratique des Hautes Etudes, Belair, Australia, May 1996.

———. "The Jewish Pasha." Unpublished manuscript. Crawford House Publishing, 1997.

Antonius, George. *The Arab Awakening: The Story of the Arab National Movement*. New York: Capricorn Books, 1965.

Asali, K . J., ed. *Jerusalem in History*. Brooklyn, NY: Olive Branch Press, 1990.

Auld, Sylvia, and Robert Hillenbrand, eds. *Ottoman Jerusalem: The Living City, 1517–1917*. Jerusalem: British School of Archaeology, 2000.

Avneri, Arieh L. *The Claim of Dispossession: Jewish Land-Settlement and the Arabs, 1878–1948*. New Brunswick and London: Transaction Books, 2002.

Baram, Uzi. "The Development of Historical Archaeology in Israel: An Overview and Prospects." *Historical Archaeology* 36, n. 4 (2002): 12–29.

Baram, Uzi, and Lynda Carroll, eds. *A Historical Archaeology of the Ottoman Empire: Breaking New Ground*. New York: Kluwer Academic/Plenum Publishers, 2000.

Be'eri, Eliezer. *The Beginnings of the Israeli-Arab Conflict, 1882–91* (Hebrew). Tel Aviv: Sifriat Poalim, 1985.

Bein, Alex. *Theodor Herzl: A Biography*. Cleveland and New York: The World Publishing Company, 1962.

Bein, Alex, ed. *Arthur Ruppin: Memoirs, Diaries, Letters*. London and Jerusalem: Weidenfeld and Nicolson, 1971.

Ben-Arieh, Yehoshua. *Jerusalem in the 19th Century: The Old City*. Jerusalem: Yad Itzhak Ben Zvi Institute, 1984.

———. *The Rediscovery of the Holy Land in the Nineteenth Century*. Jerusalem: Magnes Press, 1979.

Ben-Ezer, Ehud, ed. *Sleepwalkers and Other Stories: The Arab in Hebrew Fiction*. Boulder and London: Lynne Rienner Publishers, 1999.

Benvenisti, Meron. *Sacred Landscape: The Buried History of the Holy Land Since 1948*. Berkeley and Los Angeles: University of California Press, 2000.

Berkowitz, Michael. *Zionist Culture and West European Jewry Before the First World War*. Cambridge: Cambridge University Press, 1993.

Bloomgarden, Solomon. *The Feet of the Messenger*. Philadelphia: Connat Press, 1923.

Blumberg, Arnold. *Zion Before Zionism, 1838–1880*. Syracuse NY: Syracuse University Press, 1985.

Brenner, Yosef Haim. *Breakdown and Bereavement*. New Milford, CT: Toby Press, 2004.

Brown, L. Carl, ed. *Imperial Legacy: The Ottoman Imprint on the Balkans and the Middle East*. New York: Columbia University Press, 1996.

Campos, Michelle Ursula. "A 'Shared Homeland' and Its Boundaries: Empire, Citizenship and the Origins of Sectarianism in Late Ottoman Palestine, 1908–1913." Dissertation. Stanford University, 2003.

Campos, Michelle. "Freemasonry in Ottoman Palestine." *Jerusalem Quarterly* 22–23 (Fall–Winter 2005): 37–62.

Caplan, Neil. *Futile Diplomacy: Early Arab-Zionist Negotiation Attempts, 1913–1919*. London: Frank Cass, 1983.

Cohen, Aharon. *Israel and the Arab World*. New York: Funk and Wagnalls, 1970.

Djemal, Ahmad. *Memories of a Turkish Statesman, 1913–1919*. London: Hutchinson & Co.

Doumani, Beshara B. "Rediscovering Ottoman Palestine: Writing Palestinians into History." *Journal of Palestine Studies* 82 (Winter 1992): 5–28.

Eliav, Mordechai. *Britain and the Holy Land, 1838–1914: Selected Documents from the British Consulate in Jerusalem.* Jerusalem: Yad Itzhak Ben-Zvi Press, 1997.

Ekrem, Selma. *Unveiled: The Autobiography of a Turkish Girl.* New York: Ives Washburn, 1930.

Elon, Amos. *Herzl.* New York: Holt, Rinehart and Winston, 1975.

———. *Jerusalem: City of Mirrors.* Great Britain: Weidenfeld and Nicolson, 1990.

Elpeleg, Zvi. *The Grand Mufti: Haj Amin Al-Hussaini, Founder of the Palestinian National Movement.* London: Frank Cass & Co., 1993.

Fargo, Mumtaz A. "Arab-Turkish Relations from the Emergence of Arab Nationalism to the Arab Revolt, 1848–1916." Dissertation. University of Utah, June 1969.

Frankel, Jonathan. "The Yizkor Book of 1911—A Note on National Myths in the 2nd Aliyah." *Religion Ideology and Nationalism in Europe and America.* Jerusalem: The Historical Society of Israel and the Zalman Shazar Center for Jewish History, 1986.

Freely, John. *Inside the Seraglio: Private Lives of the Sultans in Istanbul.* New York: Penguin Books, 2000.

Fromkin, David. *A Peace to End All Peace: The Fall of the Ottoman Empire and the Creation of the Modern Middle East.* New York: Avon Books, 1989.

Furlonge, Geoffrey. *Palestine Is My Country.* London: John Murray, 1969.

Gelvin, James L. *Divided Loyalties: Nationalism and Mass Politics in Syria at the Close of the Empire.* Berkeley and Los Angeles: University of California Press, 1998.

Gilbar, Gad G., ed. *Ottoman Palestine 1800–1914: Studies in Economic and Social History.* Leiden, Netherlands: E. J. Brill, 1990.

Glass, Joseph B., and Ruth Kark. *Sephardi Entrepreneurs in Eretz Israel: The Amzalak Family, 1816–1918.* Jerusalem: Magnes Press, 1991.

Goodwin, Jason. *Lords of the Horizons: A History of the Ottoman Empire.* New York: Henry Holt and Company, 1998.

Gorenberg, Gershom. *The End of Days: Fundamentalism and the Struggle for the Temple Mount.* New York: The Free Press, 2000.

Halper, Jeff. *Between Redempton and Revival.* Boulder, San Francisco, Oxford: Westview Press, 1991.

Haslip, Joan. *The Sultan: The Life of Abdul Hamid II.* New York: Holt, Rinehart and Winston, 1958.

Herzl, Theodor. *The Jewish State*. New York: Dover Publications, 1988.

———. *Old New Land*. Princeton, NJ: Markus Wiener Pubications, 2000.

Hourani, Albert. *The Emergence of the Modern Middle East*. London: Macmillan Press, 1981.

Jacobson, Abigail. "Alternative Voices in Late Ottoman Palestine." *Jerusalem Quarterly File* 21 (August 2004): 41–48.

———. "Sephardim, Ashkenazim and the Arab Question in Pre-First World War Palestine." *Middle Eastern Studies* 39 (April 2003): 105–130.

———. "The Sephardi Jewish Community in Pre–World War I Jerusalem." *Jerusalem Quarterly File* 21 (Spring 2004): 23–34.

Kark, Ruth, and Michal Oren-Nordheim. *Jerusalem and Its Environs: Quarters, Neighborhoods, Villages, 1800–1948*. Jerusalem: Magnes Press, 2001.

Karsh, Efraim, and Inari Karsh. *Empires of the Sand: The Struggle for Mastery in the Middle East, 1789–1923*. Cambridge, MA: Harvard University Press, 1999.

Kasmieh, Khairieh. "Ruhi al-Khalidi, 1864–1913: A Symbol of the Cultural Movement in Palestine Towards the End of Ottoman Rule." In *The Syrian Land in the 18th and 19th Century*, edited by Thomas Philipp. Stuttgart: Franz Steiner, 1992.

Kayali, Hasan. *Arabs and Young Turks: Ottomanism, Arabism, and Islamism in the Ottoman Empire, 1908–1918*. Berkeley and Los Angeles: University of California Press, 1997.

Kedourie, Elie, and Sylvia G. Haim. *Palestine and Israel in the 19th and 20th Centuries*. London: Frank Cass, 1982.

Khalidi, Rashid. *Palestinian Identity: The Construction of Modern National Consciousness*. New York: Columbia University Press, 1997.

Khalidi, Rashid; Lisa Anderson; Mohammad Moslih; and Reeva S. Simon, eds. *The Origins of Arab Nationalism*. New York: Columbia University Press, 1991.

Khalidi, Rashi Ismail. *British Policy Towards Syria and Palestine, 1906–1914: A Study of the Antecedents of the Hussein–McMahon Correspondence, the Sykes-Picot Agreement, and the Balfour Declaration*. London: Ithaca Press, 1980.

———. "The 1912 Election Campaign in the Cities of Bilad Al-Sham." *International Journal of Middle East Studies* 16 (1984): 461–74.

Khalidi, Walid. "The Book of Zionism or the Question of Zionism of Muhammad Ruhi al-Khalidi, died 1913" (Arabic). *Studia Palaestina: Studies in Honor of Constantine K. Zurayk*, edited by Hisham Nashabe. Beirut: Institute for Palestine Studies, 1988.

Khalidi, Walid, and Jill Khaddon. *Palestine and the Arab-Israeli Conflict: An Annotated Bibliography*. Beirut: Institute for Palestine Studies, 1974.

Kimmerling, Baruch. *Zionism and Territory: The Socio-Territorial Dimensions of Zionist Politics*. Berkeley, CA: Institute of International Studies, 1983.

Kimmerling, Baruch, and Joel S. Migdal. *The Palestinian People: A History*. Cambridge, MA: Harvard University Press, 2003.

Kolatt, Israel. *The Hebrew Moshavot on the Eve of the First World War*. Jerusalem: Hebrew University, 1968.

Kroyanker, David. *Jerusalem Architecture*. New York: Vendome Press, 1994.

Kushner, David. *A Governor in Jerusalem: The City and Province in the Eyes of Ali Ekrem Bey, 1906–1908* (Hebrew). Jerusalem: Yad Itzhak Ben-Zvi, 1995.

———. "The Ottoman Governors of Palestine, 1864–1914." *Middle Eastern Studies* 23, no. 3 (1987): 274–90.

Kushner, David, ed. *Palestine in the Late Ottoman Period: Political, Social, and Economic Transformation*. Leiden, Netherlands: E. J. Brill, 1986.

Landau, Jacob M. *The Politics of Pan-Islam: Ideology and Organization*. Oxford: Clarendon Press, 1990.

Laqueur, Walter. *A History of Zionism: From the French Revolution to the Establishment of the State of Israel*. New York: Schocken Books, 2003.

Lasker, Michael. "Avraham Albert Antebi Chapters in His Operations in the Years 1897–1914" (Hebrew). *Pe'amim* (1984): 50–82.

Lockman, Zachary. *Comrades and Enemies: Arab and Jewish Workers in Palestine, 1906–1948*. Berkeley and Los Angeles: University of California Press, 1996.

Lowenthal, Marvin, ed. *The Diaries of Theodor Herzl*. Gloucester, MA: Peter Smith, 1978.

Ma'oz, Moshe, ed. *Studies on Palestine During the Ottoman Period*. Jerusalem: Magnes Press, 1975.

Mandel, Neville. "Attempts at an Arab-Zionist Entente, 1913–1914." *Middle Eastern Studies* 1 (April 1965): 238–68.

Mandel, Neville J. *The Arabs and Zionism Before World War I*. Berkeley and Los Angeles: University of California Press, 1976.

Mardin, Serif. *The Genesis of Young Ottoman Thought: A Study in the Modernization of Turkish Political Ideas*. Syracuse: Syracuse University Press, 2000.

Mattar, Philip. *The Mufti of Jerusalem: Al-Hajj Amin Al-Husayni and the Palestinian National Movement*. New York: Columbia University Press, 1988.

Morgenthau, Henry. *Ambassador Morgenthau's Story*. Detroit: Wayne State University Press, 2003.

Morris, Benny. *Righteous Victims: A History of the Zionist-Arab Conflict, 1881–2001*. New York: Random House, 2001.

Morris, Robert. *Freemasonry in the Holy Land*. New York: Masonic Publishing Company, 1872.

Moscrop, John James. *Measuring Jerusalem: The Palestine Exploration Fund and British Interest in the Holy Land*. London and New York: Leicester University Press, 2003.

Muslih, Muhammad Y. *The Origin of Palestinian Nationalism*. New York: Columbia University Press, 1988.

Nashabe, Hisham, ed. *Studia Palaestina: Studies in Honor of Constantine K. Zurayk*. Beirut: Institute for Palestine Studies, 1988.

Nuseibeh, Said, and Oleg Grabar. *The Dome of the Rock*. New York: Rizzoli, 1996.

Pappe, Ilan, ed. *The Israel/Palestine Question*. London and New York: Routledge, 1999.

Pawel, Ernst. *The Labyrinth of Exile: A Life of Theodor Herzl*. New York: Farrar, Straus & Giroux, 1989.

Penslar, Derek J. *Zionism and Technocracy: The Engineering of Jewish Settlement in Palestine, 1870–1918*. Bloomington and Indianapolis: Indiana University Press, 1991.

Peters, F. E. *Jerusalem*. Princeton, NJ: Princeton University Press, 1985.

Philipp, Thomas, ed. *The Syrian Land in the 18th and 19th Century: The Common and the Specific in Historical Experience*. Stuttgart: Franz Steiner Verkeg, 1992.

Podwal, Mark. *Jerusalem Sky: Stars, Crosses and Crescents*. New York: Random House, 2005.

Ramsaur, Ernest Edmondson. *The Young Turks: Prelude to the Revolution of 1908*. New York: Russell & Russell, 1970.

Ro'i, Yaacov. "The Zionist Attitudes to the Arabs, 1908–1914." In *Palestine and*

Israel in the 19th and 20th Centuries, edited by Elie Kedouri and Sylvia G. Haim. London: Frank Cass, 1982.

Rubinstein, Elyakim. "Zionist Attitudes in the Arab-Jewish Dispute to 1936." *Jerusalem Quarterly File* 22 (Winter 1982): 120–144.

Said, Edward, and Christopher Hitchens, eds. *Blaming the Victims: Spurious Scholarship and the Palestinian Question.* London and New York: Verso, 1988.

Sakakini, Khalil. "Khalil Sakakini's Ottoman Prison Diaries, Damascus (1917–1918)." *Jerusalem Quarterly File* 20 (January 2004): 7–23.

———. *Such Am I, O World: Diaries of Khalil Sakakini.* Jerusalem: Keter Publishing Company, 1990.

Schoenberg, Philip Ernest. "Palestine in the Year 1914." Dissertation. New York University, Department of History, February 1978.

Segev, Tom. *One Palestine, Complete: Jews and Arabs Under the British Mandate.* New York: Henry Holt and Company, 1999.

Shafir, Gershon. *Land, Labor and the Origins of the Israeli-Palestinian Conflict, 1882–1914.* Berkeley and Los Angeles: University of California Press, 1996.

Shapira, Anita. *Land and Power: The Zionist Resort to Force, 1881–1948.* Stanford, CA: Stanford University Press, 1999.

Shva, Shlomo, and Dahn Ben-Amotz. *Eretz Zion Yerushalayim* (Hebrew). Jerusalem: Weidenfeld and Nicholson, 1973.

Silberman, Neil Asher. *Between Past and Present: Archaeology, Ideology, and Nationalism in the Modern Middle East.* New York: Henry Holt and Company, 1989.

———. *Digging for God and Country: Exploration, Archaeology, and the Secret Struggle for the Holy Land, 1799–1917.* New York: Alfred A. Knopf, 1982.

———. "If I Forget Thee, O Jerusalem: Archaeology, Religious Commemoration and Nationalism in a Disputed City, 1801–2001." *Nations and Nationalism* 7, no. 4 (2001): 487–504.

Stein, Kenneth W. *The Land Question in Palestine: 1917–1939.* Chapel Hill and London: University of North Carolina Press, 1984.

Tamari, Salim. "Jerusalem's Ottoman Modernity: The Times and Lives of Wasif Jawhariyyeh." *Jerusalem Quarterly File* 9 (2000): 5–34.

———. "Lepers, Lunatics and Saints: Tawfiq Canaan and His Jerusalem Circle." *Jerusalem Quarterly File* 20 (2004): 24–44.

———. "The Vagabond Café and Jerusalem's Prince of Idleness." *Jerusalem Quarterly File* 19 (October 2003): 23–36.

Tamari, Salim, and Issam Nassar, eds. *Ottoman Jerusalem in the Jawharieh Memoirs: Volume One of the Memoirs of the Musician Wasif Jawharieh, 1904–1917.* Beirut: Institute for Palestine Studies, 2004.

Tauber, Eliezer. *The Emergence of the Arab Movements.* London: Frank Cass, 1993.

Tessler, Mark. *A History of the Israeli-Palestinian Conflict.* Bloomington and Indianapolis: Indiana University Press, 1994.

Teveth, Shabtai. *Ben-Gurion and the Palestinian Arabs: From Peace to War.* Oxford and New York: Oxford University Press, 1985.

Tuchman, Barbara W. *Bible and Sword: England and Palestine from the Bronze Age to Balfour.* New York: Ballantine Books, 1956.

Twain, Mark. *The Innocents Abroad.* New York: Penguin Books, 1966.

Vital, David. *Zionism: The Crucial Phase.* Oxford: Clarendon Press, 1987.

———. *Zionism: The Formative Years.* Oxford: Clarendon Press, 1982.

Wasserstein, Bernard. *Divided Jerusalem: The Struggle for the Holy City.* New Haven and London: Yale University Press, 2002.

Yehoshua, Jacob. *Jerusalem in Days of Old* (Hebrew). Jerusalem: Rubin Mass Publishers, 1981.

Index